Murder
and
Madness

❖

75 YEARS OF CRIME & PUNISHMENT ON THE PRAIRIE IN RENVILLE COUNTY, MINNESOTA

D1563597

Pat Lubeck

Patricia Lubeck

outskirts
press

Outskirts Press, Inc.
http://www.outskirtspress.com

ISBN: 978-1-9772-1548-2

PRINTED IN THE UNITED STATES OF AMERICA

TABLE OF CONTENTS

INTRODUCTION

THE MOTIVES FOR murder range from shocking to bizarre. The reason for murder is not always clear-cut, and multiple motives can be present. Here are some of the reasons for murder: financial gain, taking someone else's money from their wallet; revenge—one of the oldest reasons for murder, whether personal vendetta or long-time feud between relatives or neighbors; a heated argument over property or a personal possession; emotional murders—of greed, lust, jealousy, hatred, sadness; and mental anxiety or instability, causing momentary insanity. The list is almost endless. In this book, you will read some motives that were cause for murder in Renville County Minnesota from the late 1800s to 1940s.

All of the stories in this book are true, and many of them also involve diseases of the mind. The history of mental illness goes back as far as written records are documented. The Greek physician Hippocrates began to treat mental illness as physiological diseases rather than evidence of demonic possession or displeasure from the gods, as they had previously been believed to be. In the United States, mental illness has taken many turns and has been a journey from institutionalization of people with mental illness to moving them back into the community.

In the 1800s in the United States, people with mental illness were often incarcerated with criminals and left unclothed in darkness without heat or bathrooms; often they were chained and beaten. During this time, US reformer Dorothea Dix pushed to establish thirty-two state hospitals for the mentally ill. Unfortunately, these hospitals did not cure as previously expected, and this led to overcrowding and an emphasis on custodial care rather than humane treatment. Many mentally ill patients became homeless once they were released from the institution due to inadequate housing and follow-up care.

In modern-day treatment, new psychiatric medications have been introduced and successfully treat most people with mental illness. Very few people are committed to mental hospitals for long periods of time, due to lack of funding from private insurance companies. Homelessness and incarceration of the mentally ill continues to be a major problem, as does the lack of beds and resources to treat people with severe mental illness.

RENVILLE COUNTY HISTORY

RENVILLE COUNTY WAS established in 1855 by an act of the Minnesota Legislature. The first county election was held in 1862, but the records were lost during the US-Dakota conflict. Finally, in 1866, the county was declared organized and the second election was held. During this election, the offices of auditor, register of deeds, treasurer, sheriff, judge of probate, clerk of district court, surveyor, coroner, and county commissioners were filled. The county's present boundaries are within 982 square miles and are comprised of 27 townships and 10 cities—Bird Island, Buffalo Lake, Danube, Fairfax, Franklin, Hector, Morton, Olivia, Renville, and Sacred Heart. The county is located in west central Minnesota. The Minnesota River flows southeast along the county's southwestern border. Hawk Creek flows south through the county's western end, discharging into the Minnesota. Beaver Creek drains the central part of the county, flowing southeast before turning southwest to discharge into the Minnesota. The county terrain consists of rolling hills, and dotted with lakes and ponds. The area is devoted to agriculture.

First courthouse at Beaver Falls 1872
Photo courtesy Renville County Historical Society

In June 1871, the County Board of Commissioners appointed a building committee to oversee the building of a jail in Beaver Falls, which was the county seat at the time. The committee was authorized to procure plans and specifications, advertise and receive bids, and to secure the tract of land the jail would be built upon. Bonds were sold in the amount of $2,000 for the construction of the first jail made of stone. The small structure was completed in 1872, with court officials utilizing two rooms on one side of the building and the other side was used as the jail to board inmates. The upper floor was used as the courtroom and a meeting room for official county business.

In 1895, the city of Olivia won a battle to become the county seat, and court business was held in a local business building. Then a court decision returned the county seat to Beaver Falls for two years, but Olivia finally won the county seat permanently in 1900. Two years later, a courthouse and jail were designed by Fremont D. Orff of Minneapolis and built at a cost of $88,000. The architect combined several styles.

MURDER and MADNESS

The two stories and tower of red brick are trimmed with yellow stone that appears in quoins, belt courses, and window surrounds, as well as the central portico and solid rusticated high basement. The blue-green copper segmented domes over the corner pavilions and the central tower suggest French Second Empire. And the center pavilion with its balustered porch, fluted columns, and classic, oculus-pierced pediment is in the Georgian style. In 1933, federal money was used for repairs and redecoration of the building. Various updates and preservation projects have taken place since then. Except for different roofing material and the removal of a small spindle railing around the roof, the outside looks much as it did in 1902. The courthouse and jail were added to the National Register of Historic Places on June 13, 1986.

Renville County Courthouse, Olivia, Minnesota, 1925
Photo from Wikipedia

Renville County map, 27 townships and 10 cities

MURDER and MADNESS

JOSEPH RENVILLE

JOSEPH RENVILLE WAS born of mixed descent. His father was a French trader and his mother, Miniyehe, a Dakota (Sioux) of Little Crow's Kaposia band. She was related to some of the principal men of the Kaposia village. Renville was born at the Kaposia village about the year 1779, while the Revolutionary War was still raging. He had the daring blood of a French adventurer in one part of his lineage, and the noble strain of the Sioux in the other.

When Renville was ten years old, his father took him to Canada and placed him in the care of a Catholic priest, where he acquired a slight knowledge of the French language and the elements of the Christian religion. His education was cut short upon the death of his father, and the boy returned to Minnesota. He distinguished himself as a brave, and as he grew older, identified himself with the Dakota and married Marie (Tonkanne) Little Crow, daughter of the sister of Chief Little Crow at Prairie du Chien in accordance with Christian rites by a minister of the Catholic church. Their first child, Joseph III, was born about 1807.

Zebulon Pike, who was in Minnesota in 1805-1806, was introduced to Renville at Prairie du Chien and accompanied him to the

Joseph Renville
Photo from internet

Falls of St. Anthony. This officer was pleased with him, and recommended him for the post of United States interpreter. During the War of 1812, Colonel Dickson was employed by the British to secure the warlike tribes of the Northwest as allies. Renville was appointed the rank of captain in the British army and with warriors from the Keoxah, Kaposia, and other tribes of Dakota, marched to the American frontier. Renville was present at the siege of Fort Meigs.

For a short time after the war, Renville remained in Canada and received the half pay of a British captain. He then entered the service of the Hudson Bay Company, whose posts extended to the Mississippi and Minnesota rivers. In winter he resided with his family among the Dakota; in summer he visited his trading posts, which extended as far as the sources of the Red River.

By 1822, Renville, along with other experienced trappers, established a new company, which they called the Columbia Fur Company, located on Lake Traverse. In 1827, the American Fur Company of New York, not wanting any rivals in the trade, bought the Columbia Fur Company, but by this time, Renville had firmly established his own independent fur trading business at Lac qui Parle (near present-day Montevideo, Minnesota). He built a stockade there which became known as Fort Renville. He maintained a squad of 15-25 guards to protect himself, his property, and travelers and guests from the unfriendly Ojibwe. The guards were known as Renville's Soldiers and were also called the Tokadantee (Prairie Dogs). He lived in a log house inside the stockade. By 1832, he had ten children. In 1833, he adopted his nephew Gabriel Renville, after his only brother, Victor, was killed by Chippewa.

Renville was of a dark complexion, showing no white blood, short in stature with strong features and coarse, black hair. He was a friend

6

to the Indian, the traveler, and the missionary. He was instrumental in having the first seed corn planted on the Upper Minnesota. An Indian never left his house hungry, and they delighted to honor him.

In 1834, he met Rev. Thomas S. Williamson, a physician and missionary at Prairie du Chien. He arranged for Williamson to establish a new mission at Lac qui Parle the following year. Soon other missionaries and teachers arrived at the mission, including Rev. Stephen Riggs, Gideon Pond and his brother Samuel Pond, Rev. Thomas Longley, Alexander Huggins, Amos Huggins, and Julia LaFramboise. He worked with Rev. Riggs to translate the Bible into the Dakota language and to write a Dakota-language grammar book and dictionary.

On July 15, 1838, at Lac qui Parle, he met Joseph Nicollet, an explorer and scientist. He provided hospitality and protection for Nicollet and his group as they traveled through the area. This retreat was the only one in a 700-mile area from St. Peter to the British posts.

In 1841, Renville was chosen and ordained a ruling elder in the church at Lac qui Parle, and from that time until his death, conducted the duties of his office in a manner acceptable and profitable both to the native members of the church and the mission. After suffering from an illness for several days, Joseph Renville died on March 16, 1846. He was sixty-seven years old. He was buried at the Lac qui Parle Mission on a hilltop overlooking his stockade. His grave is unmarked. Joseph Renville earned respect that cut across the racial and ethnic boundaries of that era. The city and county of Renville were named in his honor. The Lac qui Parle Mission is a historic site and part of Lac qui Parle State Park. Fort Renville is also a historic site in Minnesota.

After his death, Martin McLeod took over the fur trade at Lac qui Parle, building his post on the southwest side of the river. Hostility to the mission increased among the Dakota once Renville's devout influence was removed. In 1854, having been largely unsuccessful, the missionaries abandoned Lac qui Parle and moved to the Upper Sioux Agency near Granite Falls, Minnesota.

FIRST LAWSUIT IN
RENVILLE COUNTY

IN THE SPRING of 1868, town meetings were held in several villages in Renville County, at which were elected peace officers, as well as other officials for the townships. This was important, in that it no longer demanded physical efforts to settle personal disputes as in years gone by. Now the strong arm of the law was prepared to lay heavy hands upon any and all criminals. In 1868, people were not overburdened with worldly goods; however, there were a few who possessed great wealth. Among them were John Tracy and Terrence Brazil, Sr.

Tracy was a quiet and industrious man; he said very little but did a lot of thinking. He brought in some stock and started to open a farm near the Birch Cooley timber. Brazil had land that ran into the timber near Tracy's. Brazil also had considerable stock and was an active, energetic man, with a growing family. He was inclined to be quick-tempered, and rather more outspoken than Tracy, but a man with generous impulses and a kind heart.

Tracy and Brazil were neighbors, but they didn't hit it off well.

Tracy's cattle would roam over Brazil's land, and Brazil's cattle would break into Tracy's field, and other things as often happen with nearby neighbors. The breach widened until finally Brazil had Tracy brought before Justice Drury on a criminal charge of cutting or mangling Brazil's cattle when they strayed over on Tracy's premises.

The case was tried at Justice Drury's house, in the north part of Birch Cooley township. E.T. Tillotson was a real character, and attorney for plaintiff Brazil, the complaining witness. Col. Sam McPhail, of Redwood Falls, another peculiar character if ever there was one, had a high-pitched voice, and appeared for the defendant, Tracy.

A jury trial was demanded, and a court officer was sent out onto the highways and tall grasses to bring in the men for a jury. Six men were all he could round up for the purpose and it was decided to go on with the case, so the six men were sworn in as jurors. The attorneys presented raging witnesses and almost came to blows themselves at times. They insisted on telling Drury what evidence to admit, and the court had its hands full keeping order and keeping the lawyers from each other's throats, insisting on preserving the dignity of the court.

Finally, the case went to the jury, who were directed to retire in charge of a bailiff to deliberate on their verdict, but there was no place to go to. The house was tiny, and a small hovel for cattle was unfit, so as a last resort, the jury of six men or boys were herded into a chicken coop so small that they had to stoop low to get in, and the odor and surroundings were something fierce, but the jury was impressed with its responsibility and did not complain about the filthy conditions. The jury believed if they said "guilty," they would send John Tracy to prison, away from his wife and family. They thought maybe Tracy had been a little hasty in firing axes, pitchforks, etc. at Brazil's cattle, even though he had some cause for wrath, but "guilty," standing out alone by itself, they could not pronounce, so the jury brought in a verdict, pronouncing Tracy guilty and imposing a fine of $40.

When the verdict was read, there was an explosion in the improvised courtroom. Col. McPhail, in his high-pitched voice, claimed the court had been insulted by the jury's trying to fine the prisoner, thus assuming a prerogative of the court. The court must have had some such idea from the way Drury expressed his surprise at the dense ignorance of law manifested by the jury. Drury ordered them to return to the coop and bring in a verdict of "guilty or not guilty," and as they were bound not to send John Tracy from his family and away to prison, they came back with a verdict of "not guilty." Then Tillotson, who didn't say much at the first verdict, set up a loud howl, but it was no use, the first lawsuit in 1868 was ended, and court was adjourned.

INCESTUOUS RAPE

HENRY KNAUF WAS born in Baden, Germany in 1830. He married Mary Ann Lewis in 1853 and settled in Montgomery, Pennsylvania in 1860. Knauf enlisted in the army on August 7, 1862, muster date August 14, 1862 at Harrisburg, PA. He was with Company A, 78th Pennsylvania Infantry. Around 1869, the family moved to Flora Township. Mary Ann gave birth to six children before her death in 1870 at the age of 39.

From the *Saint Paul Globe* newspaper, dated December 25, 1878 under the column headed "Session of Court" a case was listed as that of the State against Henry Knauf, from Renville County for trial. Presiding Judge on this case was E. St. Julien Cox, a well-read lawyer and newly appointed to the bench. This case brought a deep interest and intense feeling against the accused for the reason that the daughter of the defendant, a young but fully developed girl of sixteen or seventeen years, claimed her father had assaulted her. The charge of incestuous rape involved the most serious consequence to the defendant, if found guilty--nothing less than a life sentence.

The prosecution was conducted by county attorney Miller, and the Hon. M.G. Hanscome, an ex-judge. The evidence disclosed that the defendant, Henry Knauf, the daughter, Katherine Knauf, a son of nine or ten years, and a hired man lived out on the prairie, some distance from neighbors. During one night in May 1878, Katherine, who was asleep with her brother in the same room, awakened and found her father on top of her. Katherine swore positively to the act. There was, of course, no resistance, nor did she awaken her brother, or alarm the hired man, who slept a short distance off in a stable. She made no complaint for a week or two afterwards and the court refused to permit a medical examination to prove her chastity, as she testified that she was previously a virgin. Both Katherine and her sister, Ellen swore to acts of previous severity and cruel treatment by their father.

On the close of the case for the State, the defendant's counsel, Arctander & Griffin of Willmar, moved for his discharge. Mr. Arctander spoke on the motion some four hours, and with great ability contended for the absurdity of the charge, supporting it by an array of authorities seemingly overwhelming and convincing and displaying a research seldom seen or heard in a court of justice. The motion was overruled, and the defendant testified as to the total falsity of the charge. He also offered evidence of his good and high moral character by a number of his neighbors testifying on his behalf.

Judge Cox charged the jury very minutely as to their powers and the consideration to be given the testimony, commenting that "testimony must be of a possible, probable and rational nature, and convincingly true beyond a doubt upon which to convict." The jury retired that afternoon and remained out until the next day at noon, when they came in with a verdict of "guilty of an assault with an intent to commit a rape." A motion for a new trial had been made and taken under advisement.

It was doubtful that the conviction would stand, but it was a most extraordinary tale and shows either a depth of parental brutality and lust on the one side, or filial hatred and maliciousness on the other side, that is unparalleled in the annals of crime.

At a special term of court in January 1879, the case of Henry Knauf, charged with incestuous rape with his two daughters, aged sixteen and eighteen years respectively, came up before Judge Cox on a motion by Attorney Arctander for a new trial on the grounds that the verdict was contrary to the evidence and upon error on points of law.

Judge Cox granted the motion on the points raised, when defendant, under the advice of his attorney, withdrew his plea of "not guilty" and pleaded "guilty" to a common assault. Judge Cox sentenced Knauf to five months imprisonment in the Renville County jail. In giving evidence, the two girls said their father had told them there was no harm in it, for the Bible said it was right: "Lot and his two daughters were not punished."

Was Knauf guilty of the charge of rape with his two daughters or did they conspire against him because of their intense hatred toward their father? There was not enough evidence presented to determine who was telling the truth. This would be another case of "he said, she said," and no one was completely sure who the guilty party was in this matter. Why the defendant's attorney had Knauf change his plea from "not guilty to guilty of a common assault" is not known. This certainly adds some mystery and suspicion in this case.

Mr. Knauf got in trouble with the law a second time. William H. Schmidt, a nearby neighbor, was assaulted by Knauf with a dangerous weapon on May 8, 1883 which resulted in Knauf being held to answer before the grand jury, but Knauf furnished $250 for his bond and was released. A search was made for the court transcript on this assault charge but nothing was located, and there was nothing reported in the newspapers about this case. It could very well be that Schmidt and Knauf made amends after the assault. And Schmidt, being an honorable man, may have dropped all charges against Knauf. As we all know, neighbors sometimes have heated arguments and disagreements, but we forgive each other and life goes on.

Henry Knauf died on March 22, 1886 at the age of fifty-six and was buried at the Olivia Cemetery. His monument came through the American Legion and was placed on his unmarked grave in 1929. It doesn't appear he was buried with his wife or any of his children. What happened to Ellen and Katherine after the incest trial, one can only imagine. Ellen died in Beaver Falls 1880 at the age of twenty years. We were unable to find out what she died from. Katherine went on to get married and had two children. She died in Flora Township in 1895 at the age of thirty-three.

Henry Knauf gravestone from Find a Grave
Buried in Olivia Cemetery, Olivia, Minnesota

MURDER and MADNESS

MICHAEL J. DOWLING

MICHAEL DOWLING WAS born in Huntington, Massachusetts on February 17, 1866. His family moved frequently while he was a child and he spent time in New York, Illinois, Missouri and Wisconsin. His parents were Irish and very poor. His mother died when he was only ten years old. He sold newspapers in Chicago for a time and then came to Minnesota, where he worked on farms for two years.

On the evening of December 4, 1880, while Dowling was out tending cattle, he got lost in a severe blizzard on the prairie near Canby, Yellow Medicine County. Dowling wandered endlessly for hours, and finally, near exhaustion, found a straw stack, into which he crawled so far as his numb hands would let him. He remained there two nights and one day. When the storm abated, the boy found that he was only a few rods from the residence of Thor Landsverk on section 20, Wergeland township, Yellow Medicine County. He crawled on his hands and knees to the house and was taken care of. The boy was found to be terribly frozen and was taken to Canby.

On December 20, because of that extended exposure to cold, Dr. Andrews of Marshall, and Dr. Farnsworth of Canby operated to save his life. Both legs were amputated six inches below the knees, the left arm four inches below the elbow, and all the fingers and part of the thumb of the right hand. This all happened only a few weeks before his fifteenth birthday. The boy survived the operation and the wounds healed rapidly. Before this tragedy, Dowling had worked for three years doing farm work and herding cattle in Lyon and Yellow Medicine Counties.

After his narrow escape from death, he remained a charge upon the county of Yellow Medicine until April 1, 1883, when he made a deal with the county commissioners, where he agreed to live independently if they paid for artificial limbs for his missing legs and arm, and paid for his education at Carleton College, assuring them that if they accepted his proposition, he would never cost them another cent. By a vote of two to one, his offer was approved. To help support himself while in college, he painted fences, ran a skating rink, sold books and maps, and took any other odd jobs that he could find. Using artificial limbs, he managed to do about everything a normal person could do.

The lad who was so severely frozen in the blizzard and butchered in the resultant operation did not succumb to his misfortunes, but rapidly rose in the world. He later became a teacher in the public schools. In 1886, he worked as a school principal in Granite Falls and of the Renville schools in 1887. He held the latter position for three years and refused a flattering offer of continuance, to engage in the publication and editorship of the *Renville Star*, which he had already established. After a few months, he sold the *Star* and during the years 1890, 1891 and 1892, traveled extensively throughout the United States and Canada as a special life insurance agent. In 1892, he repurchased the *Star* and acquired the *Farmer*. He was later a banker and real estate agent in Olivia. He also became active in local Republican politics, serving as village recorder and mayor of Olivia, as well as justice of the peace for Renville County.

Dowling served as an assistant clerk in the Minnesota State House of Representatives from 1892 to 1894 and as chief clerk from 1895 to 1898. He was elected to one term as a representative, serving from 1901 to 1903. He also served as speaker of the house during that term. He was organizer of the Philippines educational system. Later he became a prominent candidate for Congress and was once nominated as a candidate for governor of the state. After World War I, he traveled to military hospitals to talk with veterans who had lost limbs, urging them not to think their lives were over.

A short silent film of Dowling was made showing how he was able to live his life normally and go about his work despite his missing limbs. The film was shown at the 1918 American Medical Association conference and has been digitized.

Dowling was an educator and legislator who succeeded in having the first bill passed providing state aid for handicapped children in 1919. Being handicapped himself, Mr. Dowling realized the importance of equal access to education for all people. The land for the Michael Dowling School built in Minneapolis was donated in 1920 by William Henry Eustis, a former Minneapolis mayor and realtor.

Dowling was a member of the Knights of Pythias, the I.O.O.F., and the A.O.U.W., the St. Paul Press Club, the Marquette Club of Chicago; was secretary of the Minnesota Editorial Association for two years; and was sent to the first national Good Roads convention at Ashbury Park in 1894, as the representative of the St. Paul Commercial Club.

Dowling was the president of the Yellowstone Trail Association in 1917. This trail system was organized in 1912 by Joseph Parmley. The trail was the first transcontinental automobile highway in the United States through the northern tier of states from Washington through Massachusetts. The motto "A Good Road from Plymouth Rock to Puget Sound" was the trail slogan, and its mission was to bring tourism to all the communities along its route.

In *The Things We Know Best*, the 1976 local history edited by Minnesota poet Joe Paddock, a woman who knew Dowling said he laughed off his handicaps. His favorite story was about the Minneapolis bellhop who, at his request, helped him get ready for bed one night. "Take of my leg," Dowling said, and the bellhop did. Then the other leg, then the arm. "Now, take my head off," he said, and the frantic bellhop ran from the room.

Dowling married Jennie L. Bordewick on October 2, 1895 in Atlanta, Georgia. Jennie was the daughter of Henry Bordewick, ex-postmaster of Granite Falls. They had three children. Dowling died on April 25, 1921; he was fifty-five years old and was buried in the Olivia Cemetery.

Dowling, age 15 after surgery and Dowling with artificial limbs
Photos from Michael Dowling School website

Dowling marker from Find A Grave, Olivia Cemetery

WIFE SLAYER

ANDREW ANDERSON LIVED with his wife, Caroline, and seven children on a farm in Henryville Township. Andrew and Caroline were born in Sweden and the families immigrated to the United States in the 1860s. Andrew was a strange character. He was often seen screaming and running around like a madman. Many of the neighbors felt he was insane.

After the harvest season, in October 1881, neighbors complained to the sheriff of Andrew's odd behavior. Andrew was served with a summons and appeared in probate court before Judge Hans Gronnerud. Andrew confessed to Gronnerud that he suffered from frequent episodes of delusions and hallucinations. Dr. Flinn of Redwood Falls and Dr. Stoddard of Beaver Falls evaluated his sanity but did not feel that his behavior required restraint at that time.

February 22, 1882 was just another day at the Anderson household. Caroline was up at the crack of dawn, stoking the fire in the old kitchen stove so she could prepare a hearty breakfast for her family. The children would be awake soon. The bedroom door was slightly ajar, and Caroline heard Andrew mumbling something as he got dressed and ready to start on the daily chores. As usual, from the bedroom,

Andrew yelled at his wife, "You got breakfast ready yet?"

"Nope, not yet," Caroline replied.

"Well hurry up, I've got work to do," Andrew screamed.

"Don't worry, you'll get it when it's ready," said Caroline.

Andrew didn't like his wife's sarcastic reply, so he immediately stormed out of the bedroom, rushed over to her, and slapped her hard across the face. Caroline had her hand on a cup of scalding hot coffee she had just poured and was ready to throw it at her husband's face, but then stopped herself, as she didn't want to cause a ruckus and wake the children. Instead she left the kitchen, went into the bedroom, and washed her face. Caroline didn't like to be anywhere near her husband when he had his fits of rage. Several minutes later, she returned to the kitchen and found an empty plate and cup on the table. It appeared Andrew had eaten his breakfast and then gone outside to tend to the animals in the barn. She was glad to be alone and rid of him for several hours. Now she could spend time getting the younger children ready for school. The children were Anton, Charles, Mathilda, John, Otto, Hilda, and Theodore. The children adored their mother but hated their father. Andrew was an abusive man that was known to beat his wife and children when he became angry. Caroline had talked to her husband about this terrible behavior many times, but it seemed as though he could not control his temper, and Caroline was at a loss as to how to rectify the situation.

It was about 6 p.m. on February 22 when Andrew finished the chores and headed for the house for supper. Mathilda, age sixteen, looked out the window and saw her father approach the house. It looked like he was carrying something, but she couldn't be sure, as it was dark outside. Finally, Andrew reached the house, opened the door, pointed a gun at Caroline, and said, "You have fooled me long enough."

Caroline grabbed at the gun, a single-barrel shotgun, but lost her grip and couldn't get it away from him. Then Mathilda took the gun away from her father and shot it off. A few seconds later, Andrew pulled out a large pocket knife, threw his wife to the floor, pulled up most of her clothes, and stabbed her several times. She asked him to let her say her prayers before he stabbed her, but he refused. Hilda and Mathilda ran to P. Shoemaker's for help and for fear that their father would hurt them, too. Caroline had a two-inch cut in her abdomen, along with other wounds and the bowels were protruding. James Doyle, a neighbor, arrived shortly after the stabbing, and found Caroline bloody and faint from the stab wounds. Doyle saw Andrew fleeing the scene, ran after him, and captured him. Andrew confessed to the deed, and was arrested and placed in the Beaver Falls jail. Drs. Flinn, Stoddard, and Hitchcock were called to attend to Caroline's wounds. She was later taken to Frederick Schmidt's residence in Flora Township to recuperate but died there five days later.

Andrew Anderson was a very cunning and slippery prisoner. On March 4, 1882, between the hours of 6 p.m. and 9 p.m., Anderson managed to escape from the jail at Beaver Falls. Somehow an ax got smuggled into his cell during the temporary absence of the jailer, and the prisoner used it to saw the bolts that were inserted into the pine framework of the door, then easily pushed the door open and walked out. There was no clue as to his whereabouts or what direction he might have taken in his flight. Several men started out about 9 p.m. that night, in search of the culprit. A $100 reward was offered by the sheriff for the apprehension and return of the fugitive.

On March 9, word was received from Redwood Falls that Anderson had been captured near Willmar and would be delivered to the proper authorities. It appeared that Anderson walked to his sister's place near Willmar—a distance of about 42 miles. He thought he could stay with her for a while, but instead, she immediately notified the sheriff and had him arrested. He was taken back to Beaver Falls by Sheriff Jensen and placed in the same cell he had escaped from a few days before.

Then in July 1882, Anderson escaped from the jail at Beaver Falls again, but about three days later, he returned voluntarily and gave himself up. Anderson said his reason for escaping was the fear of being lynched.

In October 1882, Anderson's attorney, Arctander, advised the judge that his client was insane. The attorney claimed that Anderson's son, Anton, was a material and necessary witness for the defense, without whose presence and testimony the defendant could not proceed to trial. It was said that Andrew Anderson had insane delusions of his wife's criminal conduct. He claimed that Caroline had intercourse with her sons, Anton and Charles, but of course, this never happened.

Anderson's trial was held in court at Beaver Falls in December 1882, with Judge Baldwin presiding. The best expert testimony attainable, Dr. Bartlett of St. Peter Hospital, Dr. Frost of Willmar, Dr. Puffer of St. Paul, Dr. Flinn of Redwood Falls, and Dr. Stoddard of Beaver Falls testified to Anderson's insanity, while members of his family thought him sane. However, the jury rendered a verdict of manslaughter after being out only twenty minutes. A notice of a motion for a new trial was given but was dismissed. On May 18, 1883, the judge sentenced Anderson to Stillwater State Prison for life. But on August 1, 1890, Governor William Merriam commuted his sentence on the grounds that he probably was insane at the time of the crime. Anderson was released from prison on August 1, 1891, serving only eight years of a life sentence. It was not known what became of Anderson after his release. He would have been in his sixties by then. Most of his children settled in South Dakota and Montana, so maybe he ended up living near his children somewhere, but nobody knows for sure. No Stillwater prison photos of Anderson could be located at the Minnesota History Center.

SHOT IN THE HEAD

OLE LEE, SON of Mathias Lee, living near Three Mile Creek, was in
Franklin with a load of wheat on November 20, 1882. That afternoon, as
he was leaving for home, he was approached by an eighteen-year-old youth
named Eagan, who asked the favor of a ride in his wagon, which was granted. When Mr. Lee was within a short distance of his home, Eagan repaid
the unsuspecting farmer's generosity by shooting him in the head and taking his money, $25. Eagan tied the team to a fence and then disappeared.

The murder was soon discovered, and parties started after the murderer. Eagan made his way to Fairfax on the Minneapolis & St. Louis
railroad, where he fell in with a young man named Sweeney, and they
shared one room together. The following morning, they boarded the
train for Minneapolis and Eagan was immediately arrested and turned
over to the proper authorities.

Intense indignation was manifested by the friends of the murdered
man and threats of lynching were freely made – the murder being pronounced as one of the most cold-blooded and diabolical ever made
in this part of the state. Better counsel prevailed, however, and the
murderer was taken to Beaver Falls and placed in the county jail. At

the time of his arrest, Eagan had $17.25 of the murdered man's money in his possession after paying his railroad fare, and the evidence of his guilt was so conclusive that he confessed having committed the terrible crime, but said it was done in self-defense.

Eagan worked in and around Birch Cooley and Franklin for several months, as a laborer on the railroad. Men who knew him said he had always borne a hard reputation and had bad associations. His relatives lived in Merton, Steele County.

The county jail in Beaver Falls, where Eagan was confined, was a small, square building constructed of rough fragments of stone, hastily thrown together, and into this rude pile were crowded the county offices, the courtroom, and five wooden cells. One of the occupants of the jail was Andrew Anderson, the wife-murderer, who had twice made his escape, but being a willing captive, had returned the last time of his own accord.

While the village of Beaver Falls was nestled in a gulch, the jail stood on the brow of a hill. There was a close watch kept on the jail for fear it might be attacked. A more suitable place for a lynching could scarcely be conceived. A newspaper reporter gained an interview with Eagan, and a crowd of fifteen or twenty men followed him into the jail and stood silent as grim witnesses to all that transpired. The appearance of so many men alarmed Anderson, the woman-slayer, and he shrank back as if he feared a day of reckoning, but Eagan coolly received the crowd and told the story of his monstrous deed without any hesitation.

Eagan was of medium height, sallow complexion, had bushy, coarse, black hair, large features, and would be handsome but for a dark, heavy inverted expression to the eye, which proclaimed him a fellow by the hand of nature marked, sealed, and signed to do a bloody deed.

The reporter documented Eagan's story as follows:

"My name is William Eagan, and I am 18 years of age. My father is dead, but my mother and family live at Merton in Steele

county. I went to Franklin Saturday last. I had $10 of my own money, $4 of which I spent for an overcoat and $4 for a .32-caliber revolver. Late Monday afternoon, I left Franklin and soon a man came along, whose name I do not remember, though I have heard it. He was driving a fine team and he invited me to ride. I climbed up on the seat with him and we commenced to talk about the team. He said one nag could trot a mile in 2:20 and I told him it could not be possible. He got hot and told me I was a liar. I jumped to the ground and ran. He drove his team to the fence, jumped out and ran after me. He carried a whip, caught up with me and struck me, knocking me down. Then he kicked me. He did not strike me with the butt of the whip, and his blows and kicks did not leave any marks on my body. I told him to quit and he came at me again. I tried to get up and he pushed me over. Then I shot him. The first time I fired, I thought I had missed him and so shot at him again. He never moved after that. I was lying down when I shot, and he was about a rod away from me. I went to him and found that he was dead. I took some money, which I found loose in his pocket. The purse found on me when I was searched, was my own. I don't know why I took the money from him, after I found he was dead. I thought I did right to kill him. No one saw him when he struck me or saw me when I left him, that I know of. I thought the thing would be discovered and did not try hard to get away."

Threats of lynching were made but were not executed.

At the examination proceedings, William Eagan was indicted and pled guilty to the charge of first-degree murder. There were four witnesses that testified in court on November 27, 1882.

Edward B. Jacobsen was the first witness called and his testimony follows: "I live in the town of Camp, Renville County, Minnesota. I went to Franklin Station on the 20th of November with a load of wheat and started from there about sundown. My son, Jacob, was with me and on my way home I found a dead person laying in the road with whom I am well acquainted with, whose name is Ole Lee. When I first seen him, I thought he had been hurt from the horse but on closer examination, I found a bullet hole in his head. When I found him, there was no sign of life in him and one half of his body was lying in the road, and the other half on the outside. There was a team close by him, turned into the fence, but was not tied and I tied one of them to the fence. I then removed him from the roadside but being alone with my son, I could do nothing, and left him there and went home and reported what I had seen to his father."

Karl Lee was called to the stand and stated, "Ole Lee was my brother, and he went to Franklin Station with a load of wheat on the 20th of November and on his way home, I seen him dead. When I first saw him, he was lying in the wagon box, dead, and the cause of his death, was that he had been shot, as I saw one bullet hole in his cheek."

Michel Elden testified, "I was home on the afternoon on the 20th of November 1882. I went away about sundown or a little later. I then went to Three Mile Creek and on the way down there met the prisoner and spoke to him. He said, 'Good evening' to me and I answered him the same. We spoke about the fine weather we were having, and I asked him, did I not know you, and he answered, 'No. You have never seen me before.' I have heard him speak today and the prisoner has the same voice as the person I met last night. When we parted, he went straight north toward the railroad."

John Johnson stated, "I live in the town of Birch Cooley. I heard on the evening of the 20th of November that a person by the name, Ole Lee, was killed. On the morning of the 21st, I started down on the train for Fairfax. I went down there for the purpose of catching the man whom we thought had committed this crime and we found him on the train going to Minneapolis, a little east of Fairfax. He was dressed in the same clothes that I'd seen him in a few days previous, namely in a navy-blue overcoat and a gray hat with some letters written on the visor. I and Ed Johnson, the conductor, and a few others captured him on the train and found on his person a revolver of .32-caliber six-shooter; all had been loaded but two had been shot off. The revolver was taken from him by another party, along with a pocketbook that had $17.25 in it. Afterwards he delivered to me some cartridges."

Judge H.D. Baldwin, Judge of the Ninth District Court, presided over the proceedings. The judge listened to the witness testimony, and since Eagan had plead guilty to the indictment; all that was left to do was for the judge to pass sentence upon the prisoner. The judge was a sensitive, compassionate man and took several minutes to gather his thoughts about the case. With tears in his eyes, he asked the prisoner to stand while he read the sentence. William Eagan slowly rose from his chair, tears streaming down his face. With a trembling voice the judge delivered the sentence: "You, William Eagan, having pled guilty to the charge of murder in the first degree are hereby sentenced by the court to imprisonment during the remainder of your natural life in the state prison at Stillwater, Minnesota at hard labor. Dated November 27, 1882." The judge quietly left the courtroom.

Deputy Sheriff George Miller and the prisoner left for Stillwater later that day. In years, Eagan was just a boy, and yet, so hardened had he become, that his sentence produced no visible effect on him. Eagan adapted quite well to prison life and became a model prisoner.

Ten years later, in December 1892, an application for pardon was submitted to Governor William Merriam. The pardon was initiated by H.D. Baldwin, the judge who sentenced the prisoner, S.R. Miller, the prosecuting attorney, Clark Chambers, agent for discharged convicts, and a very large number of leading and influential citizens of the state. The reasons given were that he was only eighteen years of age when the crime was committed, that it was believed he committed the murder in self-defense, that he pled guilty under the advice of his attorney, and for the reason that the people were very much exasperated over another murder in the community; and in view of these facts and the further fact of his excellent conduct in prison; the governor believed he had been sufficiently punished and the law had been fully vindicated. Governor Merriam granted a full pardon to William Eagan on December 29, 1892. Eagan was a free man after serving ten years of a life sentence. No one knows what happened to him after he left the prison yard, but it was hoped he lived a happy and prosperous life from that day forward. No Stillwater prison photos of Eagan could be located at the Minnesota History Center.

FELL IN A WELL

ON AUGUST 25, 1883, Ole Rogn Sr., of the town of Wang, told his neighbors that his wife, Gertrude, had committed suicide by throwing herself down the well; he tried to save her, but as he was pulling her up, the rope broke, and before he could get another one, she was dead. None of the neighbors seemed to doubt Ole's story as to the cause of her death. No inquest was held as there should have been, the people around there being ignorant of the law, and Gertrude was buried. But soon, there were whispers that Rogn had murdered his wife.

Rogn was known to abuse his wife, and on the morning of her death, after a heated argument, he struck her with a stove-lid, cutting a large gash in her arm, knocked her down and kicked her in the head and body, took her by the feet and dragged her around the room. Finally, Gertrude, dazed and blinded by the blood flowing from the wounds on her face, escaped from his clutches and ran out of the house, with her husband running after her. Not knowing where she was going, she fell into the open well, which was usually covered with a board. Whether Rogn made any effort to get her out was not known by the sheriff.

The entire affair was witnessed by Mrs. Anna Lumkum, who worked for Rogn, her eleven-year-old daughter, and by four or five others, but strange as it may seem, none of them ever said a word about it until sometime later. The reason they gave for not speaking out at the time was because they did not want to get into trouble and have to go to court as witnesses.

Once Rogn heard the town gossip that he was suspected of murdering his wife, he sold his farm and all his private property, and hopped on a train in Sacred Heart headed for St. Paul. Sheriff H.O. Field sent a telegram to Bird Island Sheriff's office, and when the train stopped there on its normal route, Rogn was arrested by Officer Lewis and placed in the Renville County jail to await trial.

On May 14, 1884, Rogn was arraigned on an indictment found against him and was charged with "an assault with a dangerous weapon." Rogn pled "not guilty." The case was adjourned until the next term of court. Since Rogn was unable to furnish bail, he was remanded to the county jail in Olivia.

At his trial in November of that year, Rogn withdrew his plea of "not guilty" and pled "guilty to a simple assault." The judge sentenced the defendant to thirty days in the county jail. This was certainly a light punishment for this crime, but the judge deemed the incident as a terrible accident and not an intentional homicide. No further information could be found on Ole Rogn once he left his jail cell.

A FAMILY FEUD

LINCOLN H. PARKER, a young man of twenty-two years of age, who lived in Hudson, Wisconsin, boarded a train to Hector on July 31, 1888. He was looking for a man by the name of William C. White, an attorney, who was also his brother-in-law, being married to his sister, Eva. It was well known that there was a long-standing feud between these two men, and Parker wanted to settle the quarrel once and for all.

After dinner, Parker went to White's office where they talked for about fifteen minutes. Parker threatened to shoot White, who then attempted to leave the office. Parker pulled out his revolver, fired a shot, and the ball passed through White's arm and through the hand of Emma Raitz, who was standing nearby. White ran into the post office and Parker followed and shot him through the right side. Parker was arrested and taken to the Beaver Falls jail. Dr. Murphy of St. Paul was called to attend to White and believed he would recover from his wounds.

It was reported that for a year or more, White had accused his wife, Eva, of infidelity in connection with a real estate agent in Hector. There had been a great deal of talk and scandal caused by White's accusations.

Eva White died on June 27, 1888 after giving birth to Eva, their sixth child. She was thirty-three years old, and many said that her death was hurried by White's uncalled-for charges against his wife. Mrs. White was an esteemed lady, active in church matters, and the charges were believed to have been unfounded.

Parker said that three weeks previous, while visiting his home in Hudson, White called his dead wife and family bad names and that while talking in the office on July 31, White abused him, and he lost control of himself and shot him. White denied this statement.

White was an attorney and started a campaign as a delegate to the Red Wing convention when he was shot. The public, while not defending Parker, supported him for defending his dead sister's good name.

On August 11, White died from his injuries, and Parker was indicted for murder in the first degree. Lincoln Parker applied for bail to the Hon. B.F. Webber, Judge of the 9th Judicial District, on August 16. Webber approved the application and bail was set at $10,000. Those who put up sureties for the bond were Hans Gronnerud, Jessie Brooks, David Poole and Hon. Charles D. Parker (Eva's father), former Lieutenant Governor of Wisconsin and a Regent at the University of Wisconsin.

The trial was held in Beaver Falls on October 12, 1888. Assistant Attorney General Childs and G.G. Christianson were the prosecutors, and W.W. Erwin, Mr. McLulland and S.R. Miller made up the defense. The attorneys for the defense presented a case for insanity. The trial concluded on October 16 and the case was given to the jury at 7 p.m. At 7:30 a.m., on October 17, the jury came into court and rendered a verdict of "not guilty of the crime charged in the indictment by reason of insanity." Lincoln Parker was released from custody by order of the court and walked out of the courthouse a free man. It appears Lincoln Parker committed the crime in defense of his sister's good name and reputation, and the jury deemed this horrible tragedy an act of temporary insanity. Thus, Parker got away with a cold-blooded murder.

Lincoln Parker was born in Pleasant Valley Township, St. Croix County, Wisconsin on April 2, 1860, the son of Charles D. and Angeline Parker. In July 1894, he was united in marriage to Lena Wyse of Reedsburg, Wisconsin. Mr. Parker was employed as railway mail clerk from 1886 to 1918. The couple never had any children, but in 1900 the census showed that his niece Ella (daughter of William and Eva White) and her husband Ernest Finch were living with them in St. Paul at the time. Ella would have been nine years old when her father was shot, but it appeared she didn't hold a grudge against her uncle, Lincoln, for this tragedy. Lincoln and Lena lived in Duluth for a few years and in 1918, Lincoln retired from his position with the railway and they settled in River Falls, Wisconsin.

Lincoln Parker passed away on May 26, 1954 at the Knowlton Nursing Home in River Falls. He was ninety-four years old. Funeral services were held by Finn & Segerastrom Funeral Chapel on May 28 with Rev. John Fritzmeier officiating. Internment was held in Greenwood Cemetery. The Masonic Lodge conducted burial rites at the gravesite. Mr. Parker had been a member of the local Masonic Lodge No. 109 for sixty-eight years and of the Royal Arch Masons for over fifty years. He was survived by his wife; one brother, Dr. Rupert Parker of Chicago, Illinois; and several nieces, nephews, and friends.

Lincoln Parker Monument from Find a Grave
Greenwood Cemetery, St. Croix County, Wisconsin

William White was born in 1846 to parents Oliver and Mary. In 1852, he moved with his parents to Dodge County, Wisconsin. He finished his education at the Wisconsin State University and in the fall of 1872 moved to Shakopee, Minnesota, where he taught in the grade school for one year; was principal of the Henderson schools for two years; and in 1875 was admitted to the bar in Sibley County. In 1876, he was elected county superintendent of Sibley County for two years and was justice of Henderson for four years. In 1879, he came to Hector and engaged in the practice of law; he was a member of the firm of White & Vannice. Eva A., daughter of Hon. C.D. Parker, became his wife in 1872, and they had six children: Charles O., William E., Ella A., Ethel M., Harriett M., and Eva P. William Parker was not buried with his wife. He was buried with his parents and siblings in the High Island Cemetery, New Auburn, Sibley County, Minnesota. Eva White was buried with her parents in the family plot at Greenwood Cemetery, St. Croix County, Wisconsin.

William White Monument from Find a Grave
High Island Cemetery, New Auburn, Minnesota

MURDER and MADNESS

BULLETS AND POISON

EMANUEL OTTO WAS born in 1834 in a small town in Germany. In 1854, he immigrated to Harrisburg, Pennsylvania where he worked as a carpenter. He spent some time in Iowa and Wisconsin before settling in Minnesota in 1855. He married Anna Cathrine Orth in 1857 and they had six children: Daniel (died at age five), Henry, Emily, Frederic, Anna, and William. Anna Cathrine was born on July 12, 1834 in Germany and immigrated to this country at the age of sixteen. She stayed in New York city and five years later, moved to Milwaukee, Wisconsin where she met Emanuel Otto. A few years after they were married, they moved to Minnesota, living at St. Peter and Springfield. In 1862, they moved to a farm in the Minnesota valley, a few miles from Fort Ridgely, but were hardly settled when a friendly Indian warned them of the approach of the Sioux Indians who were coming up the valley. They were advised to take the prairie trail, which they did, and with a wagon and a yoke of oxen reached St. Peter in safety. The Indians arrived on the scene soon after they left and set fire to the buildings. After the Sioux Uprising of 1862, they returned to their farm, east of Franklin, where they resided until 1893, when they retired and moved to Morton.

By 1894, Emanuel Otto was sixty years old and a wealthy farmer, living with his wife, Cathrine, about half a mile north of Morton at the foot of the bluff. He had amassed a fortune equivalent, at that time, to $100,000. Emanuel had purchased farms for all of his children and constructed houses and barns for them, while they were busy raising their own families.

It was a cold, windy day on November 14, 1894. Emanuel and Cathrine had just finished dinner. Cathrine washed the dishes and made preparations to go into town to do some shopping. Emanuel intended to go up into the ravine in back of the house to chop some wood, but as he was not feeling well the day before, Cathrine told him to lie down and take a nap instead. Emanuel told his wife he would put the key to the front door of the house under the water pail. Cathrine left the house and went to Mr. Noack's store, staying there about thirty minutes. From there she went to Fred Watschke's and stayed there quite a while. She was gone from home about two hours, and went directly home from Watschke's. As she approached the house, she noticed the front door was open. She entered and took off her hat, and thinking it quite strange that the door was open, she called out her husband's name. Hearing no reply, she stepped into the bedroom and saw him lying on the bed with his vest, shirt, trousers, woolen boots on, and truss removed. She supposed he was sleeping and attempted to wake him. She placed her arm around his neck and lifted his head up. Feeling something warm on her hand and looking at it, she saw that it was all bloody. Slowly the truth dawned upon her, and she wildly ran to the house of a neighbor, Henry Berry. Mr. and Mrs. Berry accompanied her back to the Otto residence and Dr. Penhall was summoned. The doctor arrived about 5 o'clock before the body had turned completely cold, but life was indeed extinct, and on examination, he was pronounced dead.

The doctor discovered a wound at the base of the skull at the back of the ear. An officer was placed in charge of the corpse and house, and

Coroner Stoddard was notified. He arrived and empaneled a jury. At 9 o'clock the following morning, the inquest was begun with T.M. Keefe, H.M. Noack, A. McCormick, J.M. Clancy, J.H. McGowan and Fred Storch as jury.

Drs. Flinn and Penhall made the postmortem examination of the deceased. Otto was lying on the bed with his vest, woolen shirt, pants, and drawers on. The bullet, which had passed into his left side, passed below the top of the pants, yet the only garment in which there was a hole was the woolen shirt, so that after the shot was fired the pants must have been pulled up. This is corroborated by the fact that there was some burnt powder on the drawers next to the wound. The bullet was found to have passed clear through the body, and was lying between the body and shirt on the other side. It must have been fired last, as the flow of blood from the wound was but little if any at all, the blood having rushed out of the wound in the head, before the latter shot was fired. The doctors were of the opinion that this second shot was fired after Otto was already dead. The bullet, which entered the right ear, passed just back of the ear canal, and back to the base of the brain. The canal of the wound was about two inches deep, the bullet crushing the mastoid portion of the temporal bone. The ball was found at the bottom of the wound, resting against the membrane at the base of the brain. The two bullets were found and proved to be from a .38-caliber revolver. It was Dr. Flinn's opinion that Otto was probably lying on his left side when the first shot was fired, and the course of the bullet went into Otto's ear. He declared it could not have been a case of suicide, owing to the range of the bullets.

Otto's remains were then sent to the undertaker to be dressed and prepared for burial. The funeral was scheduled for that Sunday at 10 a.m. at the Methodist Evangelical church with internment in the Morgan City Cemetery.

As the investigation during the coroner's inquest proceeded, many facts and small incidents were discovered, tending to throw suspicion on family members. The first evidence discovered was the finding of a cup in the pantry with peculiar sediment settled at the bottom. It was then that the thought of poison occurred. Sheriff William Wichman then made a search of the premises and discovered a bottle of strychnine in the outhouse vault. The contents of the cup and bottle were very similar in appearance.

Another peculiar circumstance was the testimony to the effect that the victim had just partaken of a hearty dinner, but the stomach was found to contain scarcely a tablespoonful. Suspicion pointed to poisoning. Though the poison failed to take the proper effect or possibly the victim vomited up the same (this could account for lack of food found in stomach), a revolver was used to take his life. It was thought that the shots were fired after death had occurred. The stomach was sent to chemist E.W. Young at the Minneapolis College of Physicians and Surgeons for analysis. There was suspicion and rumors floating about that William Otto, the youngest son, had purchased some strychnine poison in Franklin several months previously. To investigate this further, Coroner Stoddard and Sheriff Wichman traveled to Cornington's Drug Store in Franklin and checked the poison register, where they discovered that William Otto had indeed purchased strychnine there in May 1894. When William Otto was questioned about this evidence, he was inclined to deny that he ever bought the drug, but then his own signature was presented to him, and he finally admitted that he had bought the poison to kill some blackbirds and gophers.

The news of the previous week all tended to exonerate the Otto family, but it appeared that the jury and County Attorney Miller still had a suspicion that Mrs. Otto was in some manner involved in the crime and knew a great deal more than the jury was able to learn from her.

This suspicion arose anew when the report from State Chemist, Young was received, declaring that poison had been found in Otto's stomach. A mild solution was given to a kitten, and the animal died in forty minutes. This proved that the material discovered in the teacup on the night after the murder, by Henry Otto, who went to get a cup for the purpose of drinking, was poison. But here is where a great mystery hangs and one which is hard to solve. There were just half a dozen cups in the Otto home. The murderer must have placed strychnine in two of these cups and it must have been done with the intent of murdering both Otto and his wife. From the testimony, it was proved that Otto drank coffee for dinner on the day of the murder. The cup from which he drank the same was undoubtedly the cup from which he received a fatal dose of strychnine. The strychnine in the other cup must have been intended for Mrs. Otto, but fortunately, she got a hold of another cup in which there was no strychnine. The cup which Otto used for dinner was then thoroughly washed immediately after dinner by Cathrine and placed in the cupboard.

The theory of Dr. W.D. Flinn of Redwood Falls was that Otto felt the sickness incidental to strychnine poisoning coming on, and retired to his bed, hoping to get some relief; then the murderer, thinking Otto was not dying fast enough, went into his room and shot Otto in the ear. This done, he took the money and the key to the iron box, which Otto had in his pocket, went upstairs where he opened the box, took what he was looking for, and went downstairs again. He then passed into Otto's room and finding him in the last throes of death, presumed that he was not dying fast enough, and fired the shot into his side. That the latter shot was fired when Otto was practically dead is confirmed by the fact that no blood issued from the wound, having previously been forced out through the ear wound by convulsions produced by the strychnine poisoning.

Throughout the investigation, Cathrine Otto repeated the same details of that fateful day when she returned to the home and found her husband murdered. She persisted in saying that Otto was a perfectly happy man and loved his children dearly. A tin box where Otto kept all his valuable papers and some cash was found with the key still stuck in the lock. Mrs. Otto said that the key never left Otto's possession and she could not account for it being found where it was. And here is another mystery--in this box was $35 in currency and $5 in silver, aside from the certificates of deposit, amounting to $420. While the latter was worthless to a robber, why didn't he, if he was taking money, take the cash in the box after he had opened it? The belief is that he was frightened when he started to rob the box, and made his escape; or he secured a sufficient amount of money before he got to the bottom of the box, where the rest of the money was found.

There was some concern in determining just how Otto's arms lay when he was found. Thomas Knighton, police officer on the scene, insisted that they were folded as if prepared for death's shroud, while Dr. Penhall and Charles Berry believed that they were lying at his sides when they arrived at the scene. The latter theory was adopted. There was a search made of the premises with the hopes of finding the murder weapon or something that would lead to a clue of this mystery. Up at the top of the ravine, in a plowed area, were found foot tracks, one pair going and one pair coming, but the revolver was never found.

The sons testified that they were on their farms in Redwood County the day of the murder, had not been at the house for some time, and knew of no motive anyone would have in killing their father except for robbery. The act was shrouded in mystery at every turn; it would require some time to ferret it out, and perhaps it never would be cleared up. It was a most foul murder; it being thought he was first poisoned and then shot to cover the crime.

Authorities involved in this case were being severely censured for allowing Cashier Fred W. Orth of the Bank of Morton, who was also proprietor of the drug store in that town, to send away and get Detective B.H. Schumacher of Pinkerton Agency in St. Paul. Fred W. Orth was the nephew to Cathrine Otto. After the Otto brothers had signed the indemnity bond offering $500 as a reward for the capture of the murderer, and to assist in the prosecution of the case, Fred Orth was authorized to send for the detective. As a result, the detective stopped at Mr. Orth's house in Morton, but later registered at the Morton eating-house, evidently at the request of the jury, the members of which thought that Mr. Schumacher could do better work if he was kept away from the Orth residence.

Special Note: I contacted the Library of Congress to see if they could locate Detective Schumacher's report on the Otto case. Lara Szypszak, Reference Librarian, stated that the Pinkerton Agency collection generally consisted of main office files from New York and Chicago. Branch office files are not usually included, which explained the lack of information concerning the Minnesota case. She checked the "Criminal Case Files" in the collection, which are arranged alphabetically by case name and document type, but did not see the Otto case identified in the aid.

Fred W. Orth was born in New Ulm, Minnesota on May 21, 1866, son of Frederick and Anna (Scharf) Orth. Fred started a general store in Morton with H.M. Noack in 1887. In 1896, Fred Orth and Fred Aufderheide started a brickyard called the Morton Brick & Tile Company. After operating this for twelve years, he sold his share and in November 1891, started the Bank of Morton with Hans Gronnerud as president and Fred as cashier. In March 1908, this bank was reorganized as the State Bank of Morton, with Fred being appointed as president, Henry Beckman as cashier, and Clinton Orth (Fred's son) as assistant cashier. In company with his brother, Charles H., he also owned a stock and grain farm near Olivia, of 800 acres, 300 acres of which was used for raising corn. They fed about 100 cattle, 100 sheep, and 200 hogs per year. Fred Orth held the position of village treasurer; he was a member of the school board, and member of the I.O.O.F. On May 21, 1891, Fred married Sarah Graham, daughter of Alexander Graham, a farmer near Green Bay, Wisconsin. They had five children—Clinton, Ruby, Fred, Frank, and Helen.

Emanuel Otto did a great deal of business at the Bank of Morton. Otto was supposed to have deposited about $1,000 or more at that bank. Orth was also proprietor of the City Drug Store, and these facts caused uneasy feelings in the minds of the jury.

From the evidence deduced, Otto had certificates of deposit in Orth's bank to the extent of ten or more, nearly all being for $100 each, and of these certificates only three could be found, the total of them being $275. Otto also should have had certificates of deposit in the Redwood County Bank in Redwood Falls for $450, as the officers of that bank stated, but only one of these certificates was found, and that one was for only $100.

From the sentiment in Morton and surrounding precincts, there was a very strong feeling that Cashier Orth should be placed on the stand and made to tell all he knew regarding these missing certificates, as well as to produce his books and show the actual amount Otto had on deposit there at the time of the murder. His movements on the day of the murder should also be explained, according to popular feeling, and it was possible that when the coroner's jury would meet again, the following week, it would withdraw the verdict which it had made up to the present time and continue its investigations. The verdict, as it stood at the present time, merely found that Otto came to his death by strychnine poisoning and from two gunshot wounds from a pistol at the hands of some person unknown to the jury.

Orth's friends were indignant over the effort to implicate him and claimed that he could easily prove an alibi. Several Morton businessmen were among his friends and they were using every effort to ferret out the murderer.

On December 7, 1884, *The Morton Enterprise* included an article titled "A Scandalous Article." It seems that Julius A. Schmahl of Redwood Falls insinuated that perhaps Banker Orth had something to do with, or knew of the murder, and that he reported false information about Otto's deposits.

The following was reported in the newspaper: "Morton, MN, December 4 -- The businessmen of Morton in an indignation meeting approve the following: Whereas an article in regard to the tragic death of Emanuel Otto published in last night's Minneapolis Journal reflects upon the fair name of Fred Orth, cashier of the Bank of Morton. Resolved, that in the strongest terms we denounce such imputation against our fellow townsman as entirely unjust, unwarranted by fact or circumstance.... Orth sent for a detective only at the urgent request of the citizens and with general approval. Instead of Otto having 10 certificates at the Bank of Morton aggregating about $1,000, he simply had three, aggregating $420, and instead of deposit certificates for $450 in the Redwood County Bank, the bank officials state that he had only $100 there."

The excitement over this case continued unabated and the people of the surrounding counties appeared to take as much interest in the developments as did those located at the scene of the murder. Arrests were likely to be made at any moment.

The coroner's jury finally concluded their investigation of the Otto murder in late December. The jury had discovered nothing new and had rendered a verdict that "Emanuel Otto came to his death from two gunshot wounds, one in the ear and one in the abdomen, and strychnine poisoning; either of which would have caused death, from the hands of a person or persons to them unknown." It seems the jury, with all its endeavors to reveal the perpetrator of this crime, was unable to uncover a clue that would point to anyone sufficiently to justify an arrest. The belief of the jury as well as the community was that robbery was the possible motive for the crime, but there was no definitive proof of the culprit who committed this horrendous deed. The murderer of Emanuel Otto will probably never be known. It will pass into history as one of the most deliberate and carefully planned murder cases in this section of the state. Such a terrible death of a man who was upright, honest, and lived a true and just life.

It was reported in the *Redwood Gazette* on April 16, 1896 that Henry Otto was appointed administrator of the Emanuel Otto estate. The estate was estimated at between $50,000 and $60,000; today valued at $1,216,895. It was in mortgages, notes, real estate, and ready cash, a portion of which was found in the tin box on the second floor of the house on the day of the murder. There were five children and the widow participating in the estate. No further details were given in the distribution of assets in the estate.

In May 1899, Cathrine Otto sold the family farm to Henry Cordes for $8,000, today valued at $246,311. She then moved to Morgan where she made her home. Cathrine passed away at the home of her daughter, Mrs. Phillip Johannsen at Springfield, Minnesota on March 7, 1919. She was eighty-four years old, and was buried next to her husband in the Morgan City Cemetery.

Otto monument in Morgan City Cemetery
Photo by author

MURDER and MADNESS

BURNED ALIVE

A TERRIBLE ACCIDENT occurred on Saturday, October 30, 1897, in which a young man lost his life and brought sorrow to many hearts. Theodore Edwin was a farm laborer who was well known in the vicinity and had relatives living in Olivia.

He had just completed an engagement of farm work and intended to return to his parents' home near Norman, Iowa in a few days. He came into the village of Fairfax to attend to some business and later met up with some friends at the saloon in town and succeeded in getting intoxicated. He decided to sleep it off in the livery barn and found himself a cozy spot, lay down, and immediately fell asleep. A short while later, the marshal woke him up and placed him in jail until he became sober. The intention was to allow him to return to his friends. In placing him in the cell, the marshal searched him for weapons but no further. He was laid upon a mattress and at once fell asleep. This was around four or five o'clock in the afternoon. The jail was visited by the officer several times, and it wasn't long before he heard the snoring of the sleeping man.

About seven o'clock that evening, Lee Pullen and Carl Tolefson, at work in the warehouse less than a hundred feet away, heard some cries and upon looking toward the jail, noticed a blaze coming from a small window at the south end where the man was confined. They at once ran to the jail and bursting open the outer door attempted to reach the cell but were prevented from going any further by the smoke that poured from within and hastily gave the alarm.

The marshal was at the place in a minute. He tried to withstand the smoke and flames pouring from the cell, but fell exhausted upon the street. A line of hose was rapidly run from a hydrant to the jail in less than three minutes from the first alarm, and water poured into the cell. The fire was finally extinguished, but too late--the poor man was already dead.

Coroner Stoddard at once impaneled a jury and proceeded to carefully investigate the cause of death. After reviewing all the evidence, the jury reported "that Theodore Edwin came to his death by suffocation, caused by fire in the village jail in the village of Fairfax, Renville County, Minnesota where he was confined. The fire having the origin in the carelessness or inadvertence of Theodore Edwin and we further find that the death was in no way due to negligence or carelessness on the part of the officer. Signed by the coroner and the jurors on October 30, 1897."

News of the sad occurrence was telegraphed to the parents in Iowa, and the father and a brother-in-law arrived to take the remains home for internment. Why and how the man came to have a fire in his cell and allow himself thus to perish will always remain a mystery—whether the fire was set deliberately, intending to create an excitement and secure a release, or accidentally by embers from a lighted cigar that set the bedding ablaze, or maybe it was just from an explosion of the kerosene lamp left in the cell. How the fire started will never be known. Some money and Theodore's precious pocket watch were all that survived the fire.

VIOLENTLY INSANE

IN **1866,** THE Minnesota Legislature approved the building of a state hospital for the insane, hoping to reduce the growing number of mentally ill people in jails throughout the state. They first had to find an area willing to deed 20 acres of land for the hospital. St. Peter leaders bought a 210-acre farm for $7,000 and lent it to the state. Its first patient checked in on December 6, 1866. The hospital soon became overcrowded, so the state built three other facilities in Rochester, Fergus Falls, and Anoka. The St. Peter location remained the main hospital. Other hospitals also opened to reduce the population of patients but later closed or turned into retirement homes for the elderly. In 1911, the Asylum for Dangerous Insane officially opened on the campus of the St. Peter Hospital. Four separate institutions existed on the St. Peter campus: the mental hospital, the detention hospital, the hospital for tuberculosis insane, and the newly completed hospital for the criminally insane. The name was later changed to the Minnesota Security Hospital (MSH) in 1957. In 1982, the current MSH building opened. The original hospital has since been destroyed. One of the administration buildings has been designated as the St. Peter State

Hospital Museum.

The location of the earliest cemetery at the St. Peter State Hospital is not known. The cemetery had wooden crosses for markers and a prairie fire erased all landmarks in a large area, so the location of the cemetery was never found. The second hospital cemetery was in what is now Resurrection Cemetery; the cemetery and land on this side of the highway was later sold by the state, but the cemetery continued as a Lutheran cemetery named Resurrection Cemetery. The third cemetery is located on the grounds of the current hospital but up on top of the hill from the hospital campus. All of these graves now have monuments with names, as well as their original markers with numbers.

January 25, 1903 was a cold morning when John Wolff, his wife, and three children started in a sleigh for North Redwood where they attended church. The road they traveled passed the home of James Stephens, who was also one of their nearest neighbors. They had barely gone by the house when Marcus Stephens came out of the house, jumped on a horse and with a revolver in his hand, started in pursuit and soon gained on them. All of a sudden, he started firing into the sleigh. Mr. Wolff fell out of the sleigh. This action dazed Marcus and he stopped, not knowing what to do. But he soon continued after the sleigh, telling Wolff he would come back after him. He fired two more shots into the sleigh, or four in all, then turned back to Wolff, who in the meantime had scrambled over a wire fence and crawled into a ravine. Marcus fired two more shots at Wolff, and having no more cartridges, went back to the house.

Arthur Wolff, the young son, had received a bullet through the cap, which just grazed his forehead. John Wolff immediately contacted the Redwood authorities, who soon came to the scene of the incident.

Marcus had gone upstairs and reloaded his revolver, daring the posse to come up, saying that he would not be taken alive and would shoot the first man who appeared. Redwood's sheriff and deputy decided that to go upstairs meant certain death, so they proceeded to freeze him out and after several hours, Marcus informed them that if they would not take him out of the house until Monday, he would surrender. He laid his revolver down and backed away from it and allowed his brother to secure it. The capture was consummated. Marcus was taken to the Redwood county jail, where he remained until Monday when Sheriff Headline and Deputy Toomey drove him to Olivia. He was arraigned before Judge Gage and adjudged insane by Drs. Miller and Mesker. He was taken to St. Peter the following morning by Sheriff Headline. He remained at the insane asylum until July 1906, in for "self-abuse." He finally improved and was released a second time. We are not sure what happened to Stephens after he left the asylum.

Marcus Stephens was adjudged insane in March 1900 and sent to St. Peter. He was there until February 1901 and released. But since his return, his friends never considered him just right, although he had not been thought dangerous.

The case was a sad one, as the young man's mother died during the summer and he and his elderly father lived alone on the farm since then. Stephens' delusion was that Wolff and other of his friends were trying to kill him. He was a well-built man, twenty-nine years of age, and it would seem that his case was hopeless. This case was considered the most violent of any that had ever come before a probate judge in this county. No further information could be found on Marcus Stephens or how he spent the rest of his life.

GONE INSANE

KATE DAPPEN, DAUGHTER of John Dappen, resided on the Martin Schmitz farm in Olivia. Dappen had been working as a servant girl the past few years and had been employed in several households in Olivia. On Saturday morning, April 18, 1903, she began to show signs of mental derangement while employed at the Merchants Hotel, and in the afternoon, she went to the Silvernale home where she was employed during the winter. Here it was that the true nature of her malady was discovered, and the authorities notified.

From the ravings of the unfortunate young girl, it was surmised that a former love affair, coupled with a hereditary tendency to insanity, was the cause of the final collapse. It was known that a grandmother and uncle of Miss Dappen had gone insane. While Dappen had frequent spells of intense anger, no one thought it would prove so serious.

This last episode was very violent, and it required several men to prevent her from destroying property and injuring those who were in attendance. She had attacks of mental derangement before, but this time, her family felt she should be committed to the insane asylum. It was not known if any sort of treatment would help her condition.

Dappen was admitted to St. Peter Insane Asylum on April 20, 1903. She was accompanied to the facility by Sheriff Headline, J.L. Silvernale and Rose Dappen, her sister. A pitiful little scene was enacted at the hospital when she arrived. She imagined the nurses were nuns and that she was going to see Jesus and it gave her great joy; as she went down the corridor to her room, she was singing loudly, for to see her Lord meant freedom from all suffering, from the mental anguish, and so the doors closed upon her.

Kate was a bright child, although with a limited education and in her delirium, she spoke of the many little kindnesses done for her in the past, showing that she was alive to many of the finer feelings. We don't know if Kate spent the rest of her life in the asylum or if her mental state improved, so she could be released out into the world. No further information could be found on Kate Dappen.

ROBBERY AT DANUBE

THE PEOPLE OF the small, peaceful village of Danube were awakened at 2 a.m. on Tuesday, October 6, 1908 by loud booms caused by the explosion of nitroglyccrin coming from the State Bank of Danube, but they did not feel warranted in leaving their home and facing a gang of armed desperadoes. From reports received, it appeared that there were several members in the gang and that some of these stationed themselves on watch outside while others burglarized the vault. It was said that one man, Rev. Reed, attempted to give an alarm, but a shot was fired in his direction and he gave up further effort along that line.

It was reported that three strange men had been roaming the town and blacksmith shop the day before the robbery. Then in the early-morning hours of October 6, these same men broke into the blacksmith shop and secured a sledge, crowbar, and other tools necessary to force the door or window of the bank open for an entrance and knock the knobs off the vault and safe doors in order that they might have a small opening for the powerful explosive used. They then tried the door of the bank, as indicated by the marks of the iron bar on the wood, but failed to force it open. Then they took the screen from the north window and here they had an easy entrance.

Mr. and Mrs. Schroeder, who lived nearby, heard the racket and instinctively knew something was wrong, so they got up and dressed. Their building was so situated that the only entrance was back and front, parallel with the bank, and they rightly surmised there was trouble at the bank and that guards would be placed at front and rear so they were prisoners, as far as giving an alarm was concerned.

It seemed easy money for the bandits, as they must have spent nearly two hours in their work and made three explosions. The first one blew open the vault door, then the outer safe door, and then the "strong box." They were very likely old hands at the business, as they had their nerve right with them and did a complete job with every explosion. The vault faced the east and the last explosion was so powerful it blew the steel door to the money chest clear across the room, cutting the adding machine in two parts, and through the plate glass window, out into the middle of the street.

F.A. Schroeder, president of the bank, speaking of the loss, stated that there was $2,500 in the safe; $1,000 being in gold coin. The force of the explosion was so strong that it scattered a considerable amount of the money and destroyed some of the currency. Besides the currency, silver and pennies, there was $100 in gold left among the debris.

The strangest part of the whole affair was the fact that after working so long and making so much noise, no one seemed to even have nerve enough to watch their movements upon leaving the scene. It seemed they had those who were awake in the town terrorized, and it took some time after their departure before an alarm was sounded on the telephone.

Marshall Symes received word, surmised at once that they might have taken the morning train east, and telegraphed the conductor, reaching him at Cologne. He sent word back that three men with satchels flagged the train at Danube to get aboard, and got off at Glencoe. No one in the vicinity of Danube left town that morning, and it was highly probable these three men were the wanted bank robbers. There may have been more than three men engaged in the robbery, and a number of people seemed to think so, but the probabilities were that the three men who boarded the train were the men who did the work: a guard at front and rear, and one to do the heavy work inside.

President Schroeder lost no time in getting in communication with the First National Bank of Renville and secured enough money to keep business going as usual. Professional safe-blowers knew that country banks kept large amounts of money on hand at that time of the year to pay the farmers for their grain in moving the crop. Every year, just such banks as the one at Danube had been the victims of a raid of that kind. The bank was insured against burglary for $3,000 and that just about covered the loss. Nothing more was reported in any of the local newspapers about apprehension of the suspects, so we can only surmise that the robbers got away with the loot.

State Bank of Danube, winter 1910
Photo courtesy Renville County Historical Society

MURDER and MADNESS

DOUBLE MURDER
AND SUICIDE

THE RESIDENCE OF William Wolff in Olivia was the scene of a triple tragedy which caused the greatest sensation ever experienced in this peaceful community. Such a terrible crime had never before been committed in the county, and the stain left upon Olivia's fair name made the people deeply sensitive.

About 1 a.m. on Saturday morning, August 12, 1911, William and Mary Wolff were awakened by the cries of their daughter, Cora, who occupied an adjoining room upstairs. The girl called out to her father, "Come quick, Ed is in my room." Mary's first thought was that her daughter had been frightened by some hideous dream, and she proceeded to light the lamp while William ran to the girl's room. Just as he entered the bedroom, Mary heard the report of a revolver. She ran to the door of the bedroom and the boy told her that he would shoot her if she came into the room. She ran downstairs and out of the house to the sheriff's residence, two blocks away. She awakened Sheriff Vick, not knowing at the time that her husband was dead. Sheriff Vick called up Marshal Sherin and together they hurried to the Wolff residence.

Upon arriving at Cora's bedroom, Mr. Sherin pushed open the door part way and called to Ed to come out. The room was dark, and the marshal was unable to see anyone inside. As he called, two shots rang out in rapid succession, and thinking that the man inside was shooting at him, Sherin closed the door and retreated a few steps. When everything became quiet, he again approached the door and forced his way into the room, followed by the sheriff. As they entered the bedroom, they saw the three bodies; all were dead.

Mr. Wolff's body was lying near the door where he was shot down when he entered the room. Cora's body was at the other end of the room, and across her body lay the naked body of Edward Corey. Apparently, he disrobed himself before Cora awakened and could have raped her before he shot her. The officers immediately summoned Drs. Mesker and Hymer, who hurried to the scene of the shooting but could not detect any sign of life in any of the victims.

Mrs. Wolff, who accompanied the officers and Fred Vickstrom, night clerk at the Grand Central, to the house, became frantic with grief when she discovered the dead bodies, and her condition required the immediate attention of the doctors. She was taken to the home of William Buethe, a family friend, and cared for in every way possible.

An auto livery was sent to Hector for Coroner D'Arms, who arrived at the Wolff home shortly before 4 a.m. The coroner, along with Drs. Mesker and Hymer, made an examination of the bodies and located seven bullets. Three of these were in the body of William Wolff: one in the leg, another in the neck, and the third, which caused his death, entered his left side under the arm. Cora had two bullets in her body, one through the neck, and the other through the body, entering under the arm. In committing suicide, Corey shot himself twice in the breast, the first bullet glancing on one side of his ribs and the other proving fatal. The revolver was a .32 caliber, five chambers, and when found, contained three cartridges, showing that it had been reloaded in the room. A box of cartridges was found in the room containing thirty-nine shells.

The coroner decided that an inquest should be held. A jury was impaneled, and the inquest was held during the forenoon. The verdict was that William and Cora Wolff had been shot and killed by a revolver in the hands of Edward Corey and that Edward Corey met death by his own hand.

It seemed clear that Corey was actuated to commit the crime by a desperate love for the girl. It appeared he had been infatuated with Cora for quite some time, and although she tried repeatedly to avoid him, he continued to force his attentions upon her. They were reared in the same neighborhood and saw much of each other, but it appeared she never encouraged him in his wooing or returned his affection. While attending school at Mankato in the winter of 1910, she received a visit from him and at that time, she tried to make him understand that she did not regard him as a lover.

On the day before the murder, Corey had prepared to leave town, intending to go to Montevideo, where he had been offered a position. He left his father's home in the morning and after coming to Olivia, called at the Wolff home, presumably to say goodbye to Cora. She refused to see him, and Mr. Wolff ordered him away. Whether he made any threats at that time was not known for a certainty, but his actions were such as to alarm Cora, for shortly afterward, she went to see Sheriff Vick and informed him that she was afraid Ed would do her harm. The sheriff hunted up Ed, who was still in town, and advised him to stay away from the Wolff place, and threatened him with arrest if he should repeat his visits there. Ed promised to do as advised, saying that he intended leaving town that day. He did leave, but it appeared he went to Hector, where he remained during the afternoon, boarding the westbound evening passenger train. It was supposed he came as far as Bird Island, as he was reported to have been seen at both Hector and Bird Island that evening and that he walked from Bird Island to Olivia during the night, a distance of about five miles.

Upon arriving at the Wolff home, he took off his shoes, leaving them on the porch, and by means of a key, which he had secured in some way, gained entrance into the house. Just what his intention was in going into the house, of course, cannot be known, but it was likely that his mad love for the girl rendered him temporarily insane and that his only thought was to have his way with her and then to do away with her. The killing of Mr. Wolff was necessary for the accomplishment of the purpose in mind, and the suicide was probably an afterthought.

Both the Wolff and Corey families were old and respected residents of the community and were numbered among the best people. They lived as neighbors for many years and the most cordial relationship always existed between them.

William Wolff was born in Hopedale, Pennsylvania on January 28, 1849, and at six years of age moved with his parents to Minnesota, settling in Carver County. In the spring of 1877, he came to Renville County and took up a claim south of Olivia in Bird Island Township. In 1879, he was united in marriage to Mary Rice, and eight children were born to them. Mr. Wolff was one of the early settlers of Renville County and a pioneer citizen of the township. For thirty years, the family resided on their farm. Mr. Wolff sold his farm and in 1910 moved to town where he built a comfortable home. He was a member of the I.O.O.F. and A.O.U.W. lodges and was a stockholder in the creamery, canning factory, and Farmers Elevator Company. He was a blunt, outspoken man, but generous and kind-hearted, and honest in all his dealings. He was sixty-two years old at the time of his death.

Cora Wolff was seventeen years of age. She was born and reared in Olivia and was known as a most loveable girl. After attending some school in the country, she completed the grades in the Olivia school, and then began a business course at the Mankato Commercial College. She had a month of the course left to complete and was preparing to return to school in a few weeks when she met her untimely death. It was sad in the extreme to think this beautiful, young life was cut off in the springtime of lovely womanhood, and in a manner so deplorable and inhuman. She was the source of much comfort and joy to

William Wolff, age 62 and Cora Wolff, age 17
Photos from *The Olivia Times*, August 10, 1911

her parents, brothers, and sister and her death was a hard blow to the bereaved relatives.

Edward Corey was the second son of Adalbert and Martha Corey of Olivia. He was born near Beaver Falls and was twenty-four years old at the time of his death. He made his home in Olivia, except for a few months spent as clerk in a hotel at Montevideo in 1910. He was a quiet, unassuming young man of good habits and was never charged with an offense of any kind. That his love for the girl grew and developed into a form of madness seems evident, and it was reasonable to assume that at the time his great crime was committed, he was temporarily but completely insane. It was unbelievable that a sane mind would have done that which meant so much sorrow and suffering to the members of his own family, as well as to those of his victims. It was discovered through our research, that Jennie Estella, Edward's older sister, married Richard Wolff, Cora's older brother, but we are not sure what year they were married.

In all of Renville county there was no better citizen than the father of Edward Corey, an unfortunate young man. Adalbert Corey was a man of generous and noble impulses and was a highly respected resident in the community. The funeral of Edward Corey took place on Monday, August 7 and was attended by a large number of mourners and sympathizing friends. The services were held at the Corey home and conducted by Rev. Heard, pastor of the Methodist church. The internment was in the Olivia Cemetery in an unmarked grave.

The Wolff funeral took place Tuesday, August 8 and was one of the largest ever held in the county. The members of the Odd Fellows and Workman lodges attended. Old neighbors and friends turned out in large numbers to pay a last tribute of respect to the dead. Services were held at the home at 10 a.m. and during the hour between 10 and 11, all the business places in town were closed. From the house the remains were taken to the Moravian Church in Melville Township where services were conducted by the pastor, Rev. Newaldt and attended by the largest crowd ever assembled in that church. The internment took place at the Elim Moravian Church Cemetery in Bird Island.

This ended a tragedy in which three lives were whisked away in an instant. A culmination of a love affair when Edward Corey, a rejected suitor, shot and killed William Wolff and his daughter, Cora, who was the object of the young man's affections. The many friends of both the Wolff and Corey families in the vicinity sympathized with them in their hour of trouble, the blow to Mr. Corey, who was a close friend to Mr. Wolff, being especially severe.

CORA F. WOLFF
GEB. 24. MAI 1894.
GEST. 5. AUG. 1911.

Wolff monuments, Elim Moravian Church Cemetery
Photos from Find a Grave

CRAZY MAN

FRED ZASKE WAS born in 1866 in Germany and immigrated to this country in 1880. He first settled on a farm in Emmet Township and later moved to a farm, one-half mile south of Olivia. Fred married Martha Schmidt. They had twelve children; three of the sons—Adolph, Leon, and Walter—enlisted in WWI. Mr. Zaske had been in poor health for quite some time and acted strangely at times, but it was thought he was improving.

It was a frigid day on Thursday, December 21, 1911. That morning, the people of Olivia were startled by the fire alarm at the engine house in response to a call which came from the Fred Zaske farm. The fire department was soon at the farm with hook and ladders, pails, and other equipment. When the firemen arrived at the Zaske place, they found the barn, containing horses and cattle, almost burned to the ground. The granary and woodshed were also on fire. They learned that the fire had been started by the owner of the premises and that he was missing. They saw that nothing could be done about saving the barn, but by a little effort, the fire in the woodshed and granary was extinguished, and a search was made for the missing man.

Sometime later, Zaske was found in a well on the property, into which he evidently had jumped after torching the buildings. When discovered, he was up to his neck in water and was holding on to the piping of the pump. The firemen had considerable difficulty in getting him out, as he resisted all efforts of assistance, but finally they were able to bring him to the surface by means of hooks fastened into his clothing. He was in a frenzied and helpless condition from the effects of the excitement and the frigid water, having been in the well probably three-quarters of an hour. He was restored after some medical aid was given. He gradually recovered partially over the next several days and was eventually taken before Judge Matson, who along with Drs. Mesker and Adams, held an examination. Zaske was declared insane, committed to the asylum at St. Peter and taken to that place on December 25 by Marshal Mike Sherin.

On the morning of the incident, witnesses claimed Zaske appeared to be feeling better than usual, but after sending his two sons to the field for some hay, it appeared he became violently insane, and while in that state, committed the deed.

Mrs. Zaske claimed that her husband had been acting queerly for quite some time and had made threats that he would destroy their property. Zaske had bought an 80-acre farm adjoining his wife's property and had been brooding over the purchase. He said that he felt as though someone had hit him over the head with a club, and then did not remember anything until he was pulled out of the well.

The loss from the fire amounted to several thousand dollars, as four horses, and seven head of cattle, along with hay, harnesses, and other things, were burned with the building. Some insurance was carried with the Farmers' Mutual Insurance Company, but not enough to cover all the damages.

It was certainly the deed of a demented man, and his act of jumping into the well and refusing to be rescued would show that he was at least temporarily out of his mind. The family was grief stricken over their affliction, and they had the sympathy of the community extended to them. Mr. Zaske remained at the St. Peter asylum for treatment for a few years and was eventually released.

～⌇～

Almost seven years later, another tragedy occurred at the Zaske farm in Olivia. On November 19, 1918, at about 6:30 a.m., Martha Zaske went to the cow barn to assist with the milking. Her husband, Fred, was busy with other chores. She found her favorite stool and began milking the cows. A brief time later, Fred rushed in with an ax and attacked her, striking her in the head and cutting a deep gash near the temple, another on the top of her head and one on the back of the head. He then went to an outhouse nearby and secured a rope with which he hanged himself. When found later, by a member of the family, he was already dead. Coroner Passer and Sheriff Sunde were called, and the body was taken to the August Dirk Funeral Home and prepared for burial. The funeral was held the following day, November 20 at the funeral home.

Martha was badly injured but managed to get to the house where she was soon cared for by Dr. Passer. She received the best of attention and treatment, and finally recovered from her injuries.

That the tragedy was due to the insanity of Fred Zaske, there can be no doubt. He had been released from the St. Peter insane asylum a few years previously, and it was supposed he had recovered from his ailment, but his acts would indicate that he was seized with a sudden and violent attack. Two of Zaske's sons were with the American Army in France at the time of their father's suicide. Zaske's rash act was a sad blow to the family, and the sympathy of the community went out to them in their affliction. Fred Zaske was fifty-two years old at the time of his death.

Martha eventually moved the family to South Dakota and in the 1920 census, she still lived with ten of her twelve children. At the time of her death on April 29, 1933, she was still living with five of her children in Brown, South Dakota. She was sixty-one years old when she passed away. Fred and Martha are both buried in the Olivia Cemetery in unmarked graves.

BOXCAR MURDER

WILLIAM OLSON, A farmer from Brookfield, and two of his threshing hands left Hector on the 9:32 p.m. train to Bird Island on September 3, 1913. They were in town to purchase some parts for Olson's threshing rig. After their business was conducted, the three men had a few drinks in the local saloons, and at closing time, they bought a quart and a pint of whiskey to take back with them on the morning train. They stayed at the Bird Island Depot waiting for the train and when it started raining, they went into the boxcar to sleep until the train arrived.

At about 3:45 a.m. a man jumped into the car and waved a flashlight on the men, demanding their money. Not getting it as fast as he seemed to want it, the stranger hit one of the men over the head with the butt of his gun, got what money he had, and then got a few cents from the second man. He then went over to Olson and hit him on the head with his gun and Olson started to raise up but was shot twice in the abdomen. The stranger slowly backed up to the door, jumped out of the car, and made his escape.

The boxcar where the crime was committed stood near the PV Elevator, and Marshal Carney and Jim Peleges, engine watcher, sat on a truck at the depot but neither one heard the shots, owing perhaps to the fact that the gun was held close to the body and to the fact that it was thundering quite loudly at that time. The first they knew that anything was wrong was when they saw a man walking west along the south side of the depot. Marshal Carney called to him and the man started to run west. Owing to the fact that Marshal Carney was armed with a revolver which failed to work, neither he nor Mr. Peleges could stop the man, although both made an attempt. They then walked toward the east end of the depot and found that there had been a man murdered in a boxcar, getting this information from the two men who were with Mr. Olson. Marshal Kromer was called and others roused, but the murderer had made good his escape.

Dr. Puffer was called, but when he arrived, Mr. Olson was dead, and the body was taken to Koch's Undertaking where Coroner Passer of Olivia held an examination of the two men who were with Olson at the time of the shooting.

Sheriff Sunde and County Attorney Barnard arrived on the scene but with nothing in the way of a clue, except vague descriptions offered by those who saw the man in the car and those who saw the man who ran west from the depot, there was nothing to be done, although officers all along the line had been notified to look out for a stranger answering the description at hand, and all trains out of the village were carefully searched, and train crews notified to be on the lookout for the suspect.

A man was arrested at Olivia for robbing a blacksmith near Danube, and for a time it was thought that he was the man who did the killing, but he proved by witnesses that he was in Renville at the time, waiting to take the train east. He admitted robbing the blacksmith of $60 and the money was recovered.

An inquest was held on September 12 in Bird Island, and the jury found that William Olson came to his death from a bullet wound from a revolver in the hands of an unknown person.

The funeral was held at the Swedish Lutheran Church of Hector.

MURDER and MADNESS

Rev. J.G. Kullberg officiated, assisted by Rev. H.W. Krull of the German Lutheran Church. Internment was made in the family plot in the Hector City Cemetery.

William was born in Putnam County, New York on March 25, 1886. When he was four years old, he moved with his parents to Nicollet County, Minnesota and a year later the family moved to Renville County, where he had resided ever since. He was the son of N.W. Olson of Hector. On December 21, 1909, Mr. Olson was married to Augusta Sheiro and they had two little daughters, Ethel, age three years and Verlinda, eleven months. William was twenty-seven years old at the time of his death.

The following statement appeared in the *Bird Island Union*, September 11, 1913 as if to place blame on the victim for this terrible tragedy:

> *It was regrettable that the guilty man was not apprehended but with a gun that failed to work, neither Mr. Carney or Mr. Peleges could be blamed as they did chase the suspect for quite a distance. It was no fault of local officers and citizens that a farmer should come to town and make his bed in a boxcar and it is impossible to give police protection to those who choose such a place to sleep in, especially at this time of the year when the gunmen are being chased out of the big cities and crimes of this kind are not infrequent.*

TUBERCULOSIS
SANATORIUM

WHAT IS TUBERCULOSIS? It is an infectious disease caused by mycobacterium tuberculosis bacteria. It affects the lungs but can also affect other parts of the body. The classic symptoms of active TB are a chronic cough with blood-containing sputum, fever, night sweats, loss of appetite, fatigue, and weight loss. Historically it was called "consumption" due to the weight loss. As part of the treatment for this disease, patients were commonly sent to a sanatorium. A sanatorium was a medical facility for long-term illness, such as tuberculosis.

On September 10, 1913, a request was made by the Minnesota State Sanatorium Board to have the county of Renville, in connection with adjoining counties, build a sanatorium for tubercular patients. After considering the proposition, it was decided to employ a traveling nurse in the county for six months. The Renville County board decided to appropriate $5,000 for a tuberculosis sanatorium if Chippewa and Yellow Medicine counties would also join with them with a similar appropriation for a joint sanatorium of at least three counties. Lac qui

Parle county joined the group later.

On August 24, 1915, the bids were let for the construction and finish of the buildings that would comprise the sanatorium. The lowest bidder for the general construction work was the firm of C. Ash & Son of St. Paul, the bid being $37,500. The highest bid was $52,000. There would be three buildings on the grounds, besides the main building and power house. The former Jannusch house was rebuilt for use by the nurses.

The main building was two stories in height with a full basement, built of pressed brick. The building had a capacity of forty-four beds, besides the necessary room for the medical staff. It was felt that this sanatorium would be able to take care of the tubercular patients of the four counties. Admission to the sanatorium would be gained through the commissioners of the applicant's county. If the patient was able to pay, a moderate charge would be asked; if not able to pay, the state and county would bear the expense, the state's limit being $6 a week for each patient.

The Riverside Sanatorium opened January 1, 1917 on the bank of the Minnesota River, a very beautiful and attractive place to aid those who sought health through it. It had room for forty bed patients, with a maximum capacity of forty-eight patients; but it once housed sixty-five. A registered nurse was superintendent until 1929, with several doctors filling the post of medical director.

In 1929, Dr. Lewis Jordan was hired to fill both positions. His assistant was his wife, Kathleen, who was also a doctor. Dr. Lewis Jordan had worked with Dr. Slater at the Southwestern Sanatorium and participated in his county-wide tuberculin testing program. A similar program was instituted at Riverside, concentrating especially on Renville County, which had one of Minnesota's highest rates of tuberculosis among school-age children. Dr. Jordan's methods included tuberculin testing of all school children, teachers, staff, and school bus drivers. Those who tested positive were x-rayed, and their family members were also tested. Initially there was resistance to the TB inoculation, but by 1950, they had 100 percent cooperation in four schools. In three of the schools, no one had a positive TB reaction. It was estimated that 18,000 tests were given to children in the four counties during the program.

Dr. Kathleen Jordan worked with the state's Christmas Seal organization to test school children throughout Minnesota. She was believed to have administered 1.5 million tuberculin tests to children during her tenure. The doctors also worked with the state's health department and the US Indian Service to conduct surveys among the Dakota Indian population at Granite Falls, Morton, Redwood Falls, and Pipestone.

In June 1961, the state department of health ruled that the treatment of the water supply and sewage, both of which involved the Minnesota River, was no longer meeting standards. The sanatorium officially closed on July 1, 1963, and Dr. Jordan stayed to serve as director of the outpatient clinic until he died in 1965. The clinic remained open until 1973.

Riverside Sanatorium was the only county sanatorium that did not provide a separate house for the medical director. For thirty-one years, the Jordans lived in an apartment created for them in the nurses' building. Later the sanatorium buildings were used for an alcohol treatment program during the 1970s, but then remained empty. All the buildings on the site were finally razed in the late 1990s.

Riverside Sanatorium, Granite Falls, Minnesota
Photo from Yellow Medicine County Historical Society

MURDER and MADNESS

MURDER AND SUICIDE

ED (HENRY) BUTCHER was born in 1870 in Indiana and the family eventually settled in Renville County. He married Mary Ellen in 1895, and they had five children by 1910. However, Rita was the only one who survived. The family resided in Beaver Falls for many years. Ed was known as a quiet and unassuming farmer. He also owned a threshing company and was well thought of by all who knew him, and one of the last men anyone would pick for a desperate deed. Ed was known to have suffered from severe headaches and on some occasions, talked irrationally, but no one ever imagined it would prove serious.

On Thursday morning, January 11, 1917, the family arose early as was their custom, and about 5:30 Mr. Butcher observed his daughter, Rita, a girl of about twenty years, writing a letter to a school boyfriend. Butcher had previously objected to Rita's keeping company or corresponding with young men, and when he saw her engaged at writing, he asked her to stop doing so, but this she would not promise. He then became enraged, grabbed the shotgun, and opened fire; the first shot carried away part of the left shoulder and breast, and the other shot carried away part of the stomach, both shots striking glancingly, indicating that Rita sat with her side toward her father. He then reloaded the gun and turned it upon himself, with fatal results.

Mrs. Butcher was in the bedroom at the time of the tragedy and was uninjured. She immediately called Dr. Penhall, who contacted Mr. Fesenmair for assistance. Rita was still conscious and able to tell of the tragedy. She was rushed to Redwood Hospital for treatment but soon passed away.

During this time, Mr. Butcher's body still retained a sitting posture in his chair near the fireplace, and on the floor nearby rested the gun and empty cartridges that had taken such fearful toll of lives and wrecked an otherwise content home, which was now made desolate with this crushing blow of a double tragedy.

Rita's schoolmates could not believe the sad and calamitous news, and the community was shrouded in gloom and tender sympathy for the mother and wife who had to bear the burdens of sorrow and grief. Such a heart-wrenching tragedy, resulting from an overwrought and unbalanced mind.

Ed and Rita Butcher's markers from Find a Grave
Buried in Morton City Cemetery, Morton, Minnesota

DEADLY SHOOTING

GEORGE SCHOEPKE WAS born in Wausau, Wisconsin on June 13, 1889. He came from a large family with seven brothers and one sister: Max, Frank, Daniel, Henry, William, Ernest, Paul, and Rose. He was united in marriage to Mary Elizabeth Carlson of Renville at Olivia on May 23, 1915. They had five children: Ernest, Elsie, Claryce, George, and Mary Jane, a two-year old baby. George was engaged in farming on what was known as the Omholt farm in the valley lands adjoining the Minnesota River in western Hawk Creek Township, Renville County. George was said to be a calm, peaceful man and highly respected in the community.

On Wednesday, February 17, 1932, a shooting took place as the result of an argument over a gun. The parties involved were George Schoepke, age forty-two, and his brother, Paul, age thirty-five. It seems the two brothers had quarreled during the afternoon over getting a load of hay. George had asked Paul to help him with the work, but Paul refused. When George returned with the hay, the argument continued, and according to Elsie, age sixteen, (George's daughter), her uncle, Paul, shot at her father and told her to get into the house.

Adolph Engebretson, living nearby, heard the shots and cries for help and rushed to the assistance of the wounded man. Adolph took the wounded man to the Granite Falls Hospital where Mrs. Schoepke had been admitted the previous evening. She was seriously ill. George was still conscious when he was brought to the hospital and told his version of the whole affair to Dr. Nelson.

George had been shot four times—twice through the abdomen, once in the head, and once in the arm. He was in serious condition, according to the attending physician, and was operated on immediately to save his life. One bullet was removed from his spine after it had pierced the lung; another shot was lodged in the side of his skull; a third bullet entered his right side and penetrated the liver and could not be removed, and the fourth shot struck the man in the back of the left forearm.

Shortly after he regained consciousness, George realized the wounds were fatal and asked to see his wife and children. His five children were called to his bedside while his wife lay in an adjoining room at the hospital recovering from an operation for a ruptured appendix. George stated on his deathbed, "Paulie did it, Paulie, my brother."

George's handwritten statement of what happened the day of the shooting was found in the court transcript file of Paul Schoepke. It was written from his hospital bed on February 17, 1932 at 8:25 p.m. and listed as Exhibit H.

"Statement of George Schoepke—This afternoon I asked my brother, Paul Schoepke for a rifle that I had loaned him some time ago. Paul told me that he had hid it in one of the outhouses. I looked for it and couldn't find it. I then went out and got a load of hay on bobsled. When I got back and had unloaded the hay, I was standing on the empty sled. Paul came up and asked me if he could have my shotgun. I told him that he could not have the shotgun. The shotgun was then in the house. When I told him that he couldn't have the shotgun, Paul said, "I'm going to shoot you."

I thought Paul was fooling. Paul had a twenty-two rifle, a repeating rifle. While I was still standing on the bobsled, Paul Schoepke, my brother, shot me. The first shot was fired at me by Paul while I was on the bobsled and then I started running away from him and Paul then shot me three more times; all with said gun. I had no weapon of any kind in my hand or with me when he shot me and I did not threaten Paul in any way. Elsie came out to help me and Paul took her by the arm and led her back to the house. I am making my statement realizing that I will probably die. Signed George Schoepke"

Paul was standing in the kitchen when Sheriff Fitzner came out to the farm to arrest him. The sheriff asked him why he had done such a thing, and he answered, "Sheriff, I couldn't hold it. He was going to ram me with a fork." Schoepke took the sheriff out near the barn to show him a straw-fork on the ground which he said his brother had threatened him with. The sheriff then got the rifle from the house after Paul had looked for it under the porch and failed to find it.

Paul was immediately taken to the Granite Falls jail, but later that evening, he was transported to the Renville County jail in Olivia. When he was given his supper at the jail that evening, he said he didn't want anything as he didn't feel like eating.

Following his arrest, Paul gave the following confession:

"Statement of Paul Schoepke—I, Paul Schoepke, being informed that this statement may be used against me, make the following truthful statement of what occurred between my brother, George, and myself this afternoon. I had been living with my brother, George for about two months. We had a good many arguments between us and several times he threatened to knock my brains out. This afternoon, about two o'clock, I came into the house and was sitting there when he (George) came in and said, 'Where is that .22 rifle?' I had previously taken the rifle, which belonged to

George, and hidden it in the woods intending to sell it. I told him it was in the hen house. He then went out to look for it and came back with a chunk of wood in his hand. He said, 'You get that gun or I will use this on you'; meaning a chunk of wood. Then he tore the mackinaw (coat) off from me saying, 'This belongs to me.' Then I saw he was getting awful mad so I told him, 'Alright, I will get the gun.' Then I went towards Engebretsons, a neighbor. George went with me all the way towards Engebretsons with a stick in his hand. Then I ran away from him. Then he went back towards the house. I waited up there for quite a while, then I came back to the house. When I got back to the house he had gone for a load of hay. I went in the house and looked for my overshoes and could not find them. I then went to get the gun. I got the gun from the woods. I intended then to go to town with the gun. I then went toward the ravine. I had to go close to the house, back of the barn to get to the ravine. The ravine would have been a short cut to town, Granite Falls. Then when I came through the barnyard, he was there. When he saw me in the barnyard, he jumped off from the sleigh and said, 'Give me that gun.' He came towards me with a fork in his hand. I didn't say anything to him until he came to me with the fork. I then told him to drop that fork. He kept coming toward me. He said, 'You son-of-a-bitch, I will run this through your guts.' I then asked him where he had that shotgun. He said, 'Never mind that shotgun, give me that .22.' I then shot for his hand. He was at the time I first shot at him, about ten or fifteen feet away from me. When I shot him, he ran away from me and I shot him again. When I shot him, the second time, he was running away from me. He was running away from me toward the barn. I then shot him more times as he was running away from me. I don't remember how many times I shot. He then went towards Engebretsons and I went to the house. His little girl came out of the house after I had shot him. I had not been drinking at all today and was sober. After I shot him the first time, he ran toward the barn saying, 'I will get the shotgun and get you.'

"This statement has been read over to me before I signed it. Dated February 17, 1932. Signed Paul Schoepke"

The story told by Paul was not borne out by the facts, according to local officials who visited the scene of the crime. Shooting from the position he said he was in, the bullets could not have taken the effect they did. According to Dr. Nelson, the first bullet fired was evidently fired when George was on top of the sled, for the course of the bullet was upward after it entered the man's right side. All the other bullets struck George while he was running away from the gun.

Paul Schoepke was reported to be a shiftless character and not well-known around Granite Falls, although he had spent the winters with his brother for the last three or four years. In the spring of 1931, he was arrested and spent ten days in the county jail on a charge of drunkenness.

On February 18, 1932, Paul was interviewed by Robert Beach Henton, Esq. A portion of this interview follows:

You are here on account of this shooting deal of course as you know. As there are some questions, we want to ask you, I want to inform you that you are not obligated to answer any of them, if you don't want to. Paul Schoepke, being first duly sworn, upon oath, made the following answers to the questions set forth:

Q. Your name is Paul Schoepke? A. Yes sir.

Q. You have an older brother by name of George? A. Yes

Q. Are you married? A. No

Q. Your brother George is married? A. Yes

Q. He lives on a farm south of Sacred Heart in Renville County? A. Yes, Granite Falls.

Q. You have been staying at his farm this winter? A. Yes, for a few months.

Q. What work did you do when you were not at George's? A. Any labor I could get, anything, common labor.

Q. *Now how many are there in George's family? A. Five*

Q. *Himself, his wife and three children? A. Seven in all, he has five children.*

Q. *Did you and George ever have any arguments? A. Yes, we have had arguments before.*

Q. *Recently? A. Well, just about two weeks ago, I asked him about last winter, I was there pretty near all winter cutting wood, me and my brother Ernest cut a lot of wood there all winter, so I told him that I would like a few dollars and he told me he could not spare any then and said whenever he could sell the wood he will give me something; he said he couldn't find any place to sell the wood, that was last winter, and now when I come to Granite I heard he had been selling some wood, and when I was out there now I thought he could give me a couple of dollars.*

Q. *Did you get the money? A. No*

Q. *You still stayed there? A. I asked him for some money but he did not give me any answer, since then, he was not speaking to me, neither one was saying anything to the other.*

Q. *This .22 rifle, was that your rifle or George's? A. I really believe it belongs to Ernest.*

Q. *So far as you know, it belonged to him, you didn't own it? A. I did not own it.*

Q. *Did you ever use the rifle before this happened? A. Yes, I hunted rabbits several times.*

Q. *Why did you hide the rifle? A. When I asked him about the wood, he did not give me an answer, so I figured I would take the rifle and sell it, which I did last winter, I took some tools and sold them and got some spending money.*

Q. *You took the tools and sold them and took the money? A. Yes, I sold the tools without him knowing about it and got some tobacco money.*

Q. Did he discover that the rifle was missing? A. Yes

Q. When did he first mention that he wanted the rifle? A. Yesterday afternoon.

Q. What did he say? A. He come running to the house and said where was that rifle, I asked him what he wanted with it, and he said he wanted to go and shoot some pheasants. I told him it was out in the hen house, I had hid it in another place, when he went out there he started for the barn and when he didn't find it, he come back in and he had a chunk of wood in his hand and he said he was going to get that rifle or "I will knock your brains out."

Q. Did you know where the rifle was? A. I had on my mackinaw and was looking for my overshoes. He pulled off my mackinaw and tore off all the buttons and said it was his, and he hit me over the head with the chunk of wood, and I said, "Alright I will get the gun" and we went out and walked toward Engebretsons, and when we got over to the other side of the fence, I got away from him, he turned around and I went back toward the house and he said, "I will get the shotgun and I will get you."

Q. Where was the rifle? A. I had it in the woods there between Engebretsons and his place.

Q. After you ran away from him, then you went back home? A. Yes

Q. What did you do when he went to get the load of hay? A. I stood there by the tree a long time, I was afraid he was coming back with the shotgun, and then I went to the house to get some things that belonged to me. I took the rifle and left it by the barn and went to get my overshoes and other stuff, and when I come back, I had to go through the yard to go to the ravine to get the short-cut to town.

Q. Did you have the rifle with you? A. Yes

Q. You took it with you? A. Yes, I was going to take it with me.

Then he drove up and stopped the team and said, "Give me that rifle," and I said, "No." He dropped the lines and grabbed the pitchfork and said he was going to push the pitchfork through my guts.

Q. *How far away from you was he? A. About fifteen feet, he made a jab at me with the fork.*

Q. *Did he have the fork raised? A. Yes*

Q. *Was he pointing it ahead of him? A Yes, right toward me.*

Q. *What did he do then? A. I begged him to drop the fork. I said, "Don't do that." I told him I would shoot him if he didn't stop and I shot for his hand, and he turned and ran.*

Q. *Did you hit him the first time you shot? A. I don't know.*

Q. *How many times did you shoot? A. I don't remember, if I shot once or twice after that, I didn't mean to hit him at all, I told him not to run because I knew he was going to get the shotgun because I seen he had moved it out of the garage from where it was.*

Q. *You did not shoot at him before he got out of the sleigh? A. No. He jumped out of the sleigh with the fork in his hands.*

Q. *Did he fall down? A. No, he was right on his feet coming for me, then he started to run.*

Q. *He turned and ran after you fired the first time, you don't know if you hit him the first time you shot, but he turned and started to run? A. Yes*

Q. *He had his back to you? A. When I shot, he turned around toward the shed which was straight away from me.*

Q. *He had his back to you after that? A. Yes. He said, "I will get the shotgun and get you."*

Q. *What did you do after the shooting was all over? A. Then I went toward the house.*

Q. *Did you keep the rifle with you? A. Yes*

Q. *Where did George go? A. Toward Engebretsons*

Q. *Did he fall down? A. He got half way across over and fell down.*

Q. Was Elsie in the yard after that happened? A. No, she come outside.

Q. Did she go over to see her father at all? A. Yes, she went over there.

Q. Did you have any conversation with her? A. No, not exactly with her, she was scared. I told her I did not think I had hurt him much; I did not think he was in any danger and was not hurt much.

Q. Did she go back to the house? A. Yes

Q. Did you go back to the house with her? A. Yes

Q. You did not help him any? A. No, I wanted the shotgun, then, I wanted to end my own life.

Q. You stayed in the house after that? A. I stayed in the house after that. I was going to walk over to Granite and then I seen the car coming down the hill and I figured it was the sheriff and I come back.

Q. Were you in the house when the sheriff arrived? A. Yes

Q. Where did you get the shells for that gun? A. He bought them himself.

Q. Was it a repeating rifle? A. Yes

Q. What make was it? A. I don't know what make it was.

Q. You had it full of shells? A. I don't know how many was in there.

Q. But you got the shells out of the house? A. No, these shells were in there.

Q. In the rifle? A. Yes, we never took them out, the gun was always put up with the shells in it.

Q. Did you have any shells with you out there in the woods? A. No

Q. Did you have any in your pocket? A. No

Q. Paul, weren't you looking for that shotgun some time that day? A. No, I was looking for my overshoes.

Q. Were you looking for the shotgun after the shooting happened? A. Yes

Q. *You couldn't find it? A. No*

Q. *Were you looking for the shotgun before this trouble happened? A. No*

Q. *If you bought any shells, they were probably bought in Granite? A. I never bought any. He bought them himself.*

Q. *You don't know whether they were .22 shorts or longs? A. Longs. He got them two boxes of shells a while ago, he had some trouble with Harry Helgeson and he said he was going to get him.*

Q. *You know when he got them? A. Yes*

Q. *About how long ago was that? A. Three or four weeks ago.*

Q. *You don't know what kind of trouble he had with Helgeson? A. Yes, he had been drinking, they had gone to the neighbors and he got into an argument with George. George hit his wife and knocked her down in the snowdrift, and Harry Helgeson was along, and he called her lots of names, and Harry hit George and knocked him down. He was breaking up dishes all night. His wife and Elsie were hiding in the barn and they told me to hide the shotgun; they were afraid he was going over to shoot Helgeson.*

Q. *Was Elsie there then? A. Yes, she came out to the barn with his wife.*

Q. *Mary Schoepke, George's wife, is in the hospital now? A. Yes*

Q. *Do you know why she is there? A. No. She showed me the next day her leg and all one side was black and blue.*

Q. *Did he make any statement to you that he was getting the shells for Helgeson? A. I wasn't along over to the party. When they came back, he was talking about shooting, and the next day he got these shells.*

Q. *When he got those shells, did he say anything to you about why he got them? A. When he got home, he took them out of his pocket and said, "Here they are, now let him step into the yard."*

Q. Did he put them on the shelf? A. Yes

Q. Was there anybody else present at the time the shooting took place? A. No

Q. The only persons who possibly were present, were the children? A. No, unless the neighbors saw it.

Q. Elsie came out after it happened? A. Yes

Signed Paul Schoepke

George passed away from his wounds at 11 a.m. on Friday, February 19, 1932. He was buried in the Granite Falls City Cemetery. He was forty-two years old and left a wife and five small children behind.

George Schoepke Monument from Find a Grave
Granite Falls City Cemetery, Granite Falls, Minnesota
He is buried with two of his daughters, Claryce and Esther.

Paul Schoepke was arraigned on May 9 before County Attorney L.J. Lauerman and was charged with first-degree murder for the death of his brother, George. He pleaded not guilty and was lodged in jail to await his trial. Edward Lindquist was appointed as his counsel.

Schoepke attempted a jail break in April, a few weeks prior to the trial, but the attempt was thwarted. It appeared Paul planned well his escape, but jailer Hugo Rohner was too quick for him. When Mr. Rohner came into Schoepke's cell to remove the dinner dishes, Paul was concealed behind the cell door, armed with the leg of a chair which he had taken out for the purpose of a weapon. Just as Rohner stepped into the

MURDER and MADNESS

cell room, Schoepke swung the club, and it was about to land when a quick move by Rohner got him out of reach of the blow. In jumping away from the blow, however, Rohner left the prisoner standing between himself and the cell door, and instantly the prisoner was out of the cell. This all happened in a short space of time, but during the incident, Rohner called to his wife to lock the door leading from the kitchen into the cell corridor, which she did, just in time to prevent the escape of the prisoner. Rohner found himself locked in the cell when the prisoner left it, but he was able to direct the work of Mrs. Rohner, and in that way, hold the prisoner in the corridor. When the prisoner found that he was trapped and that any further effort at escape was useless, he opened the cell door, released Rohner, and walked back into his quarters. Charles Vosika, who was passing the jail at the time, heard the shouting of Mr. Rohner and hurried into the jail to offer his assistance, but the prompt action of Mrs. Rohner really saved the day.

The trial of Paul Schoepke began on Monday, May 16, 1932. The jury was impaneled, the work of selecting jurors occupying most of the day. Witnesses included members of the Schoepke family, Attorney Paul D. Stratton, Drs. Nelson and Sanderson of Granite Falls, Sheriff Martin Fitzner of Yellow Medicine County, and Miss Harriet Johnson, a nurse in the Granite Falls Hospital. The state offered clothing of the deceased, a bullet which had lodged in the vertebrae of the victim, the .22-caliber gun used in the shooting, several x-rays provided by Dr. Nelson, and other articles of evidence. Also, the dying man's statement was admitted into evidence, despite the vigorous protest of the defense attorney. The jury was confined to the courtroom, and jurors were not allowed to leave the building or consult with anyone concerning the case.

Mr. Schoepke appeared unconcerned at the proceedings during the trial. He had grown a heavy beard since he had been confined in jail and his face had taken on a prison pallor, making him appear unnatural. Edward Lindquist of Olivia was appointed by the court as his attorney, while County Attorney L.J. Lauerman represented the state. Judge G. E. Quale presided at the trial.

The first witness called to the stand was Mrs. Schoepke who told of being taken to the local hospital seriously ill the night before the shooting. Her husband carried her into the hospital, and that was the last time she ever saw him, for she did not leave the hospital for more than a month. Because of her medical condition, she did not know of her husband's death until a number of days after his funeral.

The daughter, Elsie Schoepke, testified about the day of the shooting. She saw the team run past the house and then saw her father stagger a few steps and fall. She ran out to help him up but was taken by the arm by Paul Schoepke and told to go back into the house.

Paul was the only one to testify on his own behalf. He stuck to his self-defense story, and at the same time, pleaded temporary insanity. He was found guilty of murder in the first degree on Thursday, May 19 in district court in Olivia. The verdict carried a mandatory sentence of life imprisonment in the state prison at Stillwater. The jury was composed of twelve men. Ole Johnson Jr. of Ericson was one of the jurors and foreman of the jury. The jurors brought in the verdict after having been out only four hours.

The defendant was brought before Judge Quale on May 20 for sentencing. The judge asked him a few questions about his parents and family life, his siblings, his schooling, his work history. He responded that he was born in Wausau, Wisconsin, left home when he was fifteen years old. His father was deceased, but his mother was still living. There were six boys and four girls in his family. His youngest brother, Ernest, was sixteen years old. He could not read or write much and was a common laborer, working on farms and lumber camps. He lived with George the past few years.

Then the judge pronounced sentence: "It is considered and adjudged that you be punished by confinement in the State Prison at Stillwater at hard labor for and during the time of your natural life."

He entered the Stillwater prison doors on May 21, 1932. The deputy warden interviewed him and we learned the following information about Paul. He was 6'1/8" tall, weighed 152 pounds, of slender

MURDER and MADNESS

build, medium-dark complexion, with black hair and grey eyes. He had a large mole under the right ear. He had a fourth-grade education and never married. His brother, William, once served a sentence for drinking.

Paul had an arrest record. In 1917, he was arrested in Lewiston, Montana (not sure of the offense) and spent thirty days in county jail. Using the alias as Fred Miller, he was arrested in Seattle, Washington March 9, 1922, on the charge of disorderly conduct and sentenced to thirty days in county jail. As Paul Schoepke, he was arrested in Minneapolis, Minnesota on November 26, 1929, on "charge investigation, disposition not given."

The deputy warden asked, "Did you have a fair trial?"

Paul's response was, "No."

The prison physician, Dr. D. Kalinoff, wrote a letter to L.F. Utecht, Deputy Warden on October 17, 1932. It read as follows: "Dear Sir, I wish to call your attention to the mental condition of Paul Schoepke. He has been acting rather peculiar for the past month and has been confined in the "Quiet Cell" at the hospital since October 13, 1932 for observation. He does not seem to remember what occurs from one day to another. Due to his mental condition, I have today recommended that he be transferred from the hospital to the Detention Ward for further observation. Signed, Very truly yours, D. Kalinoff, Prison Physician"

Paul was discharged from the Detention Ward on January 27, 1933 and transferred to his cell at the prison, but on January 30, Dr. Kalinoff wrote another letter to Deputy Warden Utecht expressing his concerns about the inmate: "Dear Sir, The actions of the inmate who was discharged from the Detention Ward and assigned to the Park on January 27, 1933, are such that would indicate that he has not fully recovered from the mental breakdown he suffered some time ago, and I recommend that he be recommitted to the Detention Ward for further observation. Signed, Very truly yours, D. Kalinoff, Prison Physician"

Paul remained in his prison cell under observation and his mental state continued to decline. Dr. Kalinoff recommended Paul be examined by a psychiatrist. On January 31, 1933, Paul was examined by a psychiatrist and his report follows: "Attitude and General Behavior—sits quietly, stares at one place, rubs his hands together and sometimes talks in a low tone. Stream of Mental Activity—is markedly slowed. He appears somewhat confused. He answers questions. Emotional Reaction—He is depressed, though he says he is not. Delusions and Hallucinations—He hears voices which come from the walls, the floor, and the ventilator in his cell. They are all right. He says he can't tell what they say. Even when he is apparently having an auditory hallucination, he will not tell what was said. Mental Grasp and Capacity—He is somewhat disoriented. He recognizes the fact that he is in prison and that certain persons are the officers of the prison but he does not recognize them nor make a clear distinction with regard to person. His memory is poor. One cannot get at his general or school knowledge, but from a previous examination, it is known to be quite limited. He has no insight. Conclusion and Recommendation—Is suffering from a psychosis. Should be examined by a commission, and if found insane, committed to the Asylum for the Dangerously Insane. Signed Psychiatrist (signature illegible)"

Paul was discharged from the Detention Ward and taken to the State Hospital at St. Peter, Minnesota on March 4, 1933. The warden sent a letter to Paul's mother, Minnie on March 6, stating "Because of your son's mental condition, it was considered advisable to transfer him to the mental hospital at St. Peter, Minnesota. Such transfer was made on March 4. Inquiries as to his welfare should be mailed to Dr. George Freeman, Supt., State Hospital, St. Peter Minnesota. You will understand that this institution is not equipped to handle mental cases and that this change has been made for your son's benefit."

Paul spent eight years and eighteen days at the State Hospital in St. Peter. We are not sure if his mother or any family members ever came to visit him there. He suffered from pulmonary tuberculosis for six years and died on March 22, 1941. He was buried in the hospital cemetery on March 24. He was forty-six years old when he passed away.

Paul's parents, Mr. and Mrs. Gustav Schoepke, had an interesting nuptial record according to *The Post-Crescent*, Appleton, Wisconsin on November 22, 1911. It stated, "They were married originally in 1886 in Wausau and are the parents of eleven children, the youngest of which is eight months. The interest lies in the fact that they were married to each other three times. This means that they were divorced twice and an action for the third divorce is now pending in the courts, the wife being the complaining witness. In each case, the husband is charged with cruel and inhumane treatment."

The Wausau Daily Herald, Wausau, Wisconsin reported the following: "In January 1912, Gustav Schoepke was in court charged with contempt in not complying with the court order regarding suit money and weekly support. He pleaded not guilty and plaintiff's attorneys were given 24 hours to file written interrogations with the clerk; then to be answered at a later date." And in May 1913, "Mrs. Wilhelmina Schoepke commenced an action for divorce in circuit court against her husband, Gustav Schoepke. At the time an order was issued by the court restraining him from visiting the Schoepke home or interfering with the plaintiff in any way. He was hauled into court charged with violating the terms of the injunction. He was found guilty of contempt of court and was sent to the county jail to serve a ninety-day term." Gustave Schoepke died in 1923 and his wife, Wilhelmina, died on April 6, 1953. They are buried in the Pine Grove Cemetery in Wausau, Wisconsin.

George and Paul lived in a dysfunctional family. They must have witnessed their father beating their mother. This may explain Paul's decision to leave home at the age of fifteen to make his own way and get away from the violence. Domestic abuse has a lasting impact on children—some develop aggressive behaviors, some abuse alcohol or drugs, and some continue the abusive cycle as adults. George was suspected of abusing his wife on many occasions. Since George saw his father beat his mother many times, he probably thought this was normal behavior.

This is a very tragic story any way you look at it. Both George and Paul witnessed domestic violence at a young age, and this impacted their lives as adults. It seemed George had an explosive temper, and Paul was probably afraid of him. This appears to be a case of self-defense, but the judge and jury didn't see it that way. Paul not only lost his brother, George, whom he loved, but also lost himself to his insanity. He suffered a fate worse than death, committed to spend the rest of his life in an asylum for the dangerously insane. Paul was merely trying to defend himself but ended up killing his beloved brother instead. The only thing that survived this terrible tragedy was one of the bullets removed from George's spine, which was used as evidence at the trial. This bullet was found in a small plastic bag in Paul Schoepke's court transcript file at the Minnesota History Center in St. Paul.

Paul Schoepke, Stillwater Prison photo, inmate #11212
Photo from Minnesota Historical Society

MURDER and MADNESS

Paul Schoepke Marker from Find a Grave
Buried in St. Peter State Hospital Cemetery
Grave #1485

MURDER ON THE
RAILROAD TRACKS

IT IS UNCLEAR exactly when hobos first appeared on the American rail-roading scene. With the end of the Civil War in the 1860s, many discharged veterans returning home began hopping freight trains. Others looking for work on the frontier followed the railways west aboard freight trains in the late 19th century. In 1906 there were about 500,000 transients, and by 1911, it was estimated the number had surged to 700,000. The number of hobos increased greatly during the Great Depression era of the 1930s. With no work and no prospects at home, many decided to travel for free by freight train and try their luck elsewhere.

Life as a hobo was dangerous. In addition to the problems of being poor and far from home and support, plus the hostility of many train crews, they faced the railroads security staff, nicknamed "bulls," who had a reputation of violence against trespassers. Riding a freight train was dangerous in itself. Many lost a foot, or worse, when they fell under the wheels trying to jump aboard a train. It was easy to be trapped between cars, and one could freeze to death in bad weather.

When freezer cars were loaded at an ice factory, any hobo inside was likely to be killed.

The hobo jungle was a place of refuge and rest while on the road. It was like a campsite, with big open fire pits set up along the rails, but secluded, where the hobo could eat, sleep, read a newspaper, wash himself, and do his laundry before heading out again. The jungle was close enough to get to and from the train yard or rail line, but not so close as to attract unwanted attention. Accessibility to the railroad was just one of the requirements for a good jungle. It was usually located in a dry and shady area that permitted sleeping on the ground. There needed to be plenty of water for cooking and bathing and wood enough to keep the pot boiling. If there was a general store nearby where bread, meat, and vegetables could be had, so much the better.

Jungle camps were divided into two classes: the temporary and the permanent. Temporary jungles were just stop-overs inhabited by men temporarily stranded and seeking a place to layover without being molested by authorities or criminals. In places where the trains stopped frequently, these camps tended to become more permanent.

In the following story, there was one such "jungle camp" along the train tracks in Sacred Heart. This place was well-known among the locals and was designated "Hobo Park" in the 1930s. Recently, a friend of mine took me to the very place where this "hobo park" once existed. Of course, nothing remains of the campsite. But for me, it was like stepping back in time; I could just imagine the poor, destitute hobos living in this quiet, picturesque, secluded spot along the tracks so many years ago. What happened here in September 1936, involved two friendly hobos (also known as transients). It's a heartbreaking story, and one you will never forget.

A transient spent part of the night camped out with a group of men along the tracks near the stockyards in Sacred Heart. At about 2 a.m.

he left the camp and said to his companions, "I am going to catch a train going west." When he did not return, the men took it for granted that he had hopped a freight and was on his way.

Later that morning, on September 13, 1936, one of the men came upon the transient's mangled body. The remains were spread many yards between the rails. It was probable that both east and westbound trains passed over the body.

Coroner L.R. Pirsch of Olivia was called and pronounced the death accidental. The body was taken to Nordstrom and Sagnes Mortuary and on Monday afternoon was buried in an unmarked grave at the Sacred Heart City Cemetery. Rev. T.H. Rossing conducted a service at the gravesite.

Nothing was found on the man's clothing or body to give a clue as to his identification. He had a little over five dollars in cash in his pockets. Fingerprints were taken by the coroner, which were sent to Washington for possible identification by the Veterans' Bureau or the Department of Justice. Railroad investigators working on the case were of the opinion that the man laid himself or was placed between the rails by his assailant at a point 350 feet east of the stockyards and directly behind the Gilbert Hagen residence. The theory was that he was struck by the westbound train passing through at 2:39 a.m. and not by the eastbound train, which goes through that area much earlier.

Joseph Williams was a transient who had befriended the man whose remains were found along the tracks that day. He spoke with investigators during the morning but left Sacred Heart later that day and continued westward to Huron, South Dakota where he found employment with a man named Joe Reilly.

The death was termed accidental until Joe Williams talked too much at Huron and was turned over to the authorities. Williams claimed that his companion of several weeks on the road gave him his money just before he committed suicide at Sacred Heart. The incident seemed to have been weighing heavy on the man's mind so that he talked of it incessantly to his employer, Joe Reilly, who was suspicious of his story and reported it to the sheriff of Beadle County, South Dakota. The sheriff was eager to investigate the matter and accompanied Reilly to his home, where Williams was arrested and placed in the Beadle County Jail in Huron. Sheriff Heaney of Renville County was notified of the incident.

A few days later, Sheriff Heaney made the trip to Huron to question the man and bring him back to Renville County to prepare more serious charges against him. It was thought that Williams might have murdered his companion to get his money from him and then thrown his body on the tracks to make it look like a suicide.

When Heaney entered the prisoner's cell to question him, he could see that Williams was suffering from a mental breakdown. He was confused, talking incessantly, and pacing back and forth in the small space. It appeared that this terrible tragedy was a heavy burden on his mind. Heaney took custody of Williams and they traveled to Renville County the following day, where he was placed in the county jail in Olivia.

The prisoner repeatedly denied any crime, but finally cracked under the grilling he was put through at the sheriff's office. In an eleven-page confession signed on September 30, 1936, in the presence of County Attorney Russell L. Frazee, Sheriff Henry Heaney, and John Burns of the Criminal Bureau of Apprehension of Willmar; Joe Williams finally admitted slaying his transient companion at the local stockyards on September 13. Below is a portion of his eleven-page confession:

> *Mr. Frazee to Mr. Williams:*
> *Now Joe, I am going to ask you some additional questions here and I want to first inform you that you don't have to answer them unless you want to, and if you do answer them, it is understood by you that you are answering them of your own free will and accord.*
> *Q. You understand that? A. Yes*
> *Q. We are going to start with by asking you if you were present the morning the Coroner came down to Sacred Heart to view the body of the man that was found scattered along the tracks,*

were you present that morning in Sacred Heart? A. Yes

Q. *You were there? A. Yes*

Q. *Did you talk to the Coroner? A. No, I went down to the box-car.*

Q. *You talked to the Coroner when he was down that morning? A. Yes*

Q. *You were out to the tracks and saw the scattered body of this man? A. Yes*

Q. *Now the evening before this morning, did you eat supper there in the jungles with the man? A. Yes, supper in the jungles.*

Q. *He was the only one there besides yourself? A. Yes, but of course there was some—I was the only man there.*

Q. *He was the only man there with you? A. Yes*

Q. *Did you go up town there and get something to eat that night for both of you? A. Well I kind-a think I did.*

Q. *Didn't he give you twenty or twenty-five cents and send you up town to get some bologna and other groceries? A. Yes*

Q. *How much did he give you? A. He gave me 25 cents.*

Q. *You went up town? A. Yes*

Q. *What did you buy? A. I bought bologna and I bought two loaves of bread.*

Q. *You brought that back with you? A. Yes, I got two, I believe I bought some apples.*

Q. *What time of the day was this? A. Oh, it was in the evening.*

Q. *About what time? A. Oh, along towards night time.*

Q. *Was it dusk? A. Yes*

Q. *The sun had gone down? A. Not quite.*

Q. *After you got back to the jungles with this bologna, apples, and two loaves of bread, did you and this man that was with you prepare and eat it? A. Yes*

Q. *Where did you eat it? A. On this here –*

Q. *A platform? A. A platform right out there at the stockyards.*

Q. *You sat down there on the platform at the stockyards and ate it? A. Yes*

Q. *When you finished eating, where did you go? A. Well—*

Q. *Did you go back to the jungles? A. I went back to the jungle for a while.*

Q. *Did he go with you? A. No not quite, no.*

Q. *Where did he go? A. He sat around there for a while.*

Q. *What did you do at the jungles? A. I didn't do it at the jungles.*

Q. *Did you pick up something at the jungle? A. Scrap iron.*

Q. *You picked up a piece of iron? A. Yes*

Q. *Will you describe that piece of iron for us? Look at that piece of iron, Joe (Sheriff produces iron bolt). That is a heavy bolt is it not? It is about 14" long? A. Yes, it is heavy. I suppose it is about that long.*

Q. *About an inch in diameter? A. Yes*

Q. *Is that the piece of bolt you picked up? A. Yes*

Q. *What did you do with that piece of bolt, did you put it in your pocket? A. Yes*

Q. *Which pocket? A. This here one (indicating).*

Q. *In your right rear overall pocket? A. Yes*

Q. *You came back to the platform? A. Yes*

Q. *Was this man still sitting there? A. Well for a while, yes.*

Q. *Did you and he go together then? A. Yes*

Q. *How long was this after you finished eating? A. Oh, about an hour, I guess.*

Q. *So, by that time the sun had gone down and it was dark? A. Yes*

Q. *You and he were the only two around? A. Yes, at that time I think it was.*

Q. *Did he show you his pocketbook? A. Yes, he showed me the pocketbook.*

Q. *You saw he had a considerable amount of money in the pocketbook? A. Yes*

Q. *Now after you came back from the jungles with this piece of iron in your pocket, what did you do if anything, or what did he do or say? A. He said he was going; he was just going to take the train.*

Q. *Did he say which direction he was going? A. He said he was going east.*

Q. *Did he carry his jacket in his arms? A. Yes*

Q. *You described him the other day as being a big man? A. Yes, he was pretty good size.*

Q. *How much would you say he weighed? A. Gosh, I don't know; he was a pretty good size.*

Q. *About how old would you say he was? A. Around forty-five, forty or forty-five, something like that.*

Q. *Did he tell you during the time you and him were together where he was from? A. No*

Q. *Did he say anything at all about his family? A. Not about his family to me at all.*

Q. *So, you don't know, didn't know that evening, and don't know now who he was or where he was from, is that correct? A. I never heard his name at all.*

Q. *Do you know where he was from? A. No, I don't know.*

Q. *He told you where he had worked or who he had worked for? A. I believe he told me once where he had worked but I can't remember.*

Q. *Now after you got back from the jungles with this piece of iron in your pocket and after he had told you he was going to take an east-bound train, and then started leaving, and he proceeded to walk towards the tracks in a southerly direction and what did you do then? A. Well I went along too, I followed after him.*

Q. *You followed right behind him? A. Yes*

Q. *How far did you follow him? A. Oh, I did not follow very far.*

Q. *Would you say ten feet, fifteen feet? A. About that.*

Q. *Then what did you do? A. So, I knocked him down.*

Q. You what? A. I hit him with this iron.

Q. Where did you hit him? A. (indicating)

Q. In the back of the head? A. Yes

Q. When you hit him with that, did he fall down? A. Yes, he fell down.

Q. How many times did you hit him? A. I hit him twice.

Q. After you hit him the first time, did he fall down? A. No, the second time.

Q. What did he say after you hit him the first time? A. He did not say anything.

Q. Didn't he let out an exclamation? A. He said "Oh," something like that.

Q. You hit him again? A. Yes, and then he fell down.

Q. How far was that from the main track there when he fell? A. He wasn't so very far.

Q. There are two main tracks there? A. Yes

Q. There is a siding or switching track that runs close to the stockyards? A. Yes

Q. There is another track or the main track, just south of that track? A. Yes

Q. You are referring now to the main track as being the track on which he fell? A. Yes

Q. Now after he had fallen, what did you do? A. When he fell, I just drug him onto the track.

Q. You remember whether you laid him lengthwise down on the track or cross-wise? A. No, I don't know, I never stayed, I walked away.

Q. Well, didn't you take this money from him? A. That money I got that night.

Q. You got that after you knocked him twice on the head? A. Yes

Q. You took that money before you put him on the track? A. Yes

Q. Do you remember which direction his head was facing? A. No, I don't know.

Q. Will you tell us just how you pulled him onto the track? A. Well, I just took him like this (indicating on Mr. Burns).

Q. You grabbed him by the shoulders? A. By the shoulders, yes.

Q. Was the entire part of his body in between the tracks? A. As far as I can remember, it was.

Q. When did you first get the idea that you were going to rob him? A. Well, I just got it in there.

Q. Was it while you were going up town after these groceries? A. Yes

Q. When you left him there at the platform and went down to the jungles alone, was your reason in doing that to go down there and get a piece of iron? A. Well, I went down there to get a piece of iron.

Q. When you went down to the jungles, you decided to pick up this piece of iron that you have identified as being the one you hit him over the head with, is that right? A. Yes

Q. Do you know whether he was dead when you pulled him onto the track? A. Well, I wouldn't say for sure, because I put him on the track and left.

Q. Was he pretty still? A. Pretty still, yes.

Q. You told us this morning when you put him onto the tracks that he was dead. Were you correct when you told us that this morning? A. He was dead when I put him onto the track?

Q. He was? A. Yes

Q. You are sure of that? A. Yes

Q. You have seen dead persons before? A. Yes, sir.

Q. And you are positive he was dead when you pulled him onto the tracks? A. Yes

Q. Why did you pull him onto the tracks, Joe? A. Well, I just figured on getting him on the tracks.

Q. You did that to cover up, didn't you? A. Yes

Q. You did that so it would appear that he had fallen off the train and had been run over? A. Yes, sir.

Q. *After you pulled him onto the tracks, where did you go? A. Well, I went down to the boxcar then.*

Q. *Which direction was that from where you left him on the tracks? A. That boxcar was a ways-back.*

Q. *Back east or west? A. Back west.*

Q. *How far? A. Oh, about three or four cars.*

Q. *Did you crawl into that boxcar? A. Yes*

Q. *Did you remain there the rest of the night? A. Yes*

Q. *Do you remember any trains passing there shortly after you had left him on the tracks? A. The first train passed shortly after I left.*

Q. *How soon afterwards? A. It wasn't so very long.*

Q. *Half an hour? A. About half an hour, I guess.*

Q. *Was that a freight or passenger? A. A freight.*

Q. *You are sure about that? A. Yes*

Q. *You are sure it wasn't a passenger? Did you see it go by? A. Well, I am pretty sure it was a freight train.*

Q. *You are not sure, you could not see it? A. I am pretty sure it was, of course it was dark.*

Q. *Were you inside the boxcar when the train went by? A. Yes*

Q. *Was the south side of the boxcar open? A. Yes*

Q. *Did you stand there near the door and watch the train go by? Where were you at in this boxcar when the train went by? Were you lying down? A. I stood up alright.*

Q. *In the door and watched the train go by? A. Yes*

Q. *So, you would know whether it was a freight or passenger? A. Pretty sure it was a freight train.*

Q. *Did you know a freight train was coming along when you placed his body on the tracks? A. No*

Q. *You slept in the freight car all night? A. In the car, yes.*

Q. *The next morning you knew someone had found his body scattered along the tracks? A. Yes*

Q. *That was the morning you talked with the Coroner? A. Yes*

Q. *He asked you if you knew who the fellow was? A. Yes*

Q. *You told him you didn't, is that right? A. Yes*

Q. *All that time you had his money in his purse in your pocket, is that right? A. Yes, that is right.*

Q. *You did not tell the Coroner about that, is that right? A. No, I did not tell the Coroner.*

Q. *How long did you stay there that morning, Joe? A. Oh, I stayed there about, probably half a day, maybe.*

Q. *When did you leave, did you leave around noon. A. I left around noon.*

Q. *Which direction did you go? A. I was going west.*

Q. *How did you leave? Did you start walking down the tracks and catch a freight or passenger train? A. I started walking out of town.*

Q. *Along the track or road? A. I started up the railroad tracks.*

Q. *How far did you get up the railroad tracks before you caught a freight or train? A. I did not catch a freight, I just went on the train tracks until I came to a highway crossing it, and then I went on the highway and walked.*

Q. *You walked up the railroad tracks a short distance, how far? A. I hit the highway quite a ways out.*

Q. *Was it one or two miles? A. About three miles.*

Q. *How long did you walk along the highway? A. I took the highway and kept to it all the way.*

Q. *Did you walk all the way to Huron? A. Not all the way, pretty near it.*

Q. *You did catch an occasional ride? A. Yes, but I first walked and then I would catch rides.*

Q. *You went to Aberdeen? A. Yes, I went to Aberdeen first.*

Q. *You went to Aberdeen from Sacred Heart? A. Yes*

Q. *How long did you stay in Aberdeen? A. I stayed there a couple of days.*

Q. *From there where did you go? A. I come on down to Redfield.*

Q. From Redfield where did you go? A. From Redfield I went to Huron.

Q. How did you get from Aberdeen to Redfield? A. Well, I started out on foot.

Q. You "hitch-hiked" a ways, caught a ride and then you would walk? A. I caught a ride on the highway into Redfield.

Q. Then did you follow the same procedure of travel from Redfield to Huron, by catching rides and by walking? A. By the highway.

Q. After you got to Huron, what did you do? A. Well, I stayed there again for a while.

Q. How long? A. I remember the day was on the Fair Day.

Q. At Huron? A. Yes, the Fair Day.

Q. Do you know a man by the name of J.M. Bussel? A. Let's see, that doesn't sound familiar to me.

Q. That is the name of the man to whom you gave the pocketbook with $200 in it? A. Yes

Q. Where did you meet him? A. Well, I met him about 30 miles, he told me he lived 30 miles from Huron.

Q. Did you meet him at Banila, South Dakota? A. Yes, it was a little town.

Q. He is the one to whom you gave this pocketbook with the money in it. How much money was in the pocketbook? A. He counted it; said it was $200.

Q. Had you spent any of this money from the time you had taken it from this man at Sacred Heart until you gave it to Mr. Bussell at Banila? A. $10

Q. So, there was approximately $210 in the pocketbook when you took it off of this man at Sacred Heart, is that correct? A. Yes. Then this fellow who counted it, I gave him $5, this Bussell.

Q. Did you give it to him or did he just take it? A. He took it.

Q. What did he take it for? A. Well, I don't know.

Q. Did he tell you he was going to take out $5? A. He said he would just take out $5.

Q. *Showing you this brown leather pocketbook—is this the pocketbook that you took from this man in Sacred Heart after you struck him over the head? A. Yes, that is the pocketbook.*

Q. *That is the pocketbook that had the money in it that you gave to Bussell? A. Yes*

Q. *Do you remember or recall whether or not there was any cards or paper in this pocketbook with any names on it? A. There was a slip right in there.*

Q. *Was it a card or a piece of paper? A. Just a piece of paper.*

Q. *Did it have something written on it? A. It looked like a name.*

Q. *Do you remember what the first part of the name was? A. I don't remember, he took it to read it.*

Q. *Who took it? A. Bussell*

Q. *What did he do with this piece of paper? A. Tore it up.*

Q. *Did you see him tear it up? A. Yes, we both did.*

Q. *Did he say anything to you about keeping the money? A. He said, "Let me take this money and put it in the bank." He does his business in the First National Bank.*

Q. *Do you know whether he put it in the bank? A. Well, he come back with a deposit slip that he was showing; I don't know for sure whether he put it in the bank, but he went away with it.*

Q. *How was this man dressed at Sacred Heart that was with you, the man you knocked over the head? A. He was dressed in overalls, he had a pair of overalls on, and a pair of pants under the overalls.*

Q. *He had a pair of trousers on under the overalls? A. Looked like moleskins.*

Q. *Did he have on low ankle shoes or high shoes? A. He had on low ankle shoes.*

Q. *Were they oxfords? A. No, not oxfords.*

Q. *They were something like the ones you got on? A. Yes, they wasn't high boots.*

Q. *Where did he have this pocketbook with the money in it? A. In his pocket.*

Q. *Of his overalls, the front pocket of his overalls? A. Yes*

Q. *Did you search him for anymore pocketbooks? A. No*

Q. *Did you know that he had another pocketbook with money in it on him? A. No, I never knew it.*

Q. *Did he have any jewelry on him, such as watches, rings? A. Yes, he had a watch.*

Q. *Did you take it? A. No*

Q. *What kind of a shirt was he wearing? A. He was wearing a brown flannel.*

Q. *Brown color? A. Yes, but it was an older shirt; I got this shirt and underwear in Aberdeen, South Dakota.*

Q. *Did you stab him with his knife before you threw him on the track there, Joe? A. No, I did not stab him with no knife.*

Examination continued by John Burns of Criminal Bureau of Apprehension of Willmar, Minn.

Q. *You say you bought that shirt and underwear at Aberdeen? A. Yes, sir.*

Q. *What money did you use to buy that with? A. Well, let's see, I used that $10.*

Q. *$10 that you took out of the pocketbook? A. Yes, I spent $5 of that.*

Q. *How long had you been with this man before you hit him? A. I had been with him probably two days.*

Q. *Two or three days? A. Yes*

Q. *How long had you been in the jungles there at Sacred Heart? A. Just one day.*

Q. *During this particular evening that you hit him, was there anyone else in or around the jungles there with you? A. No*

Q. *All of those other men were back in the jungles? A. Yes*

Q. *You did not know any of them? A. No, I did not know any of them.*

Q. You have not made this statement that you made to the County Attorney, to the Sheriff or myself here, because you were forced to make it, have you? A. No

Q. Why are you making it? Has this thing been bothering you since it happened? A. Yes, it has been bothering me.

Q. You are making this statement to clear the situation up and get it off you mind? A. Yes, to clear the thing up and get it off my mind.

Q. You are making it freely and voluntarily? A. Yes

Q. Did you and this man have some beer? A. No, I bought some beer.

Q. You bought some beer with his money? A. Yes, of course I have bought two or three cigars along about that time.

Q. Also using his money? A. Why yes, also.

I, Joe Williams have read the above questions and answers, and state that the answers as given to the questions herein contained, are all true, that said answers have been given by me of my own free will and accord without any promise or coercion or threat of violence. Dated at Olivia, Minnesota, this 30th day of September 1936.

Signed: Joe Williams
Witnesses: Russell Frazee and Henry Heaney

Williams was held on a charge of first-degree murder and would be brought before a special grand jury to be called before his trial at the fall term of the district court. On November 27, a sanity hearing was held in Probate Court for Williams. At that time, he was adjudged sane, and was bound over to the court to await his trial.

Williams trial was held on December 19, 1936. He was convicted by a jury of first-degree murder of a transient, and Judge Baker sentenced him to spend the rest of his life in Stillwater State Prison. He was immediately transported to the state prison at Stillwater, and the deputy warden interviewed Williams when he arrived that evening. The following details were revealed about the prisoner—Williams was born in Cass County, Missouri about 1876. He was 60 years old when he committed the crime. Joseph was 5'5" tall, weighed 112 pounds and of a slender build. He had a fair complexion, gray balding hair, and blue eyes. He had a scar on the left side of his chin, on the outside corner of his left eye and running under the left eye. He drank liquor to excess and smoked tobacco. He completed the second grade and left school when he was seven years old. He was single. He had two step-brothers and one sister, Mrs. Ida Mulcahey who lived in Pittsburg, Kansas. He left home when he was fourteen years old to find work and make his own way in life. In 1934, he was arrested for vagrancy in Sioux City, Iowa and spent one night in jail. He worked in most every state in the Midwest but held no job longer than three or four months. He was employed as a farm hand, laborer, followed the harvest, etc. He could not remember any names of former employers. He stated that he was in Minnesota only a few hours before the crime was committed. After he was interviewed, he was given his prison uniform and escorted to the cell he would call home for the rest of his life.

The resident prison physician, Dr. Gunnar Linner, wrote the following letter to L.F. Utecht, Deputy Warden on December 31, 1936, expressing his concerns of prisoner, Joseph Williams. "Dear Sir, this man has been in the Detention Ward for several days, and was placed there because of peculiar actions displayed. He is disoriented, his mind wanders from the subject of conversation and he does not even remember where he is or why he is here. I advise keeping him in observation cell until further diagnosis of his mental condition can be established. Very truly yours, Dr. G. Linner"

Williams continued to act peculiar and disoriented through the month of January 1937. He was examined by three doctors and their report follows: "To the Honorable: The State Board of Control, St. Paul, Minnesota: Examination was made at the Prison on the morning of January 27, 1937, and the following history was obtained. A note by Deputy Warden Utecht on December 27, 1936, states that "this man's behavior is unusual, the direct result, I believe of an unsound mental condition. It is necessary that one guard watch him at all times. He is unable to find his way around the institution alone and appears to be in somewhat of a daze at all times. A note by the night Captain on December 29, 1936, indicates that Williams #13401 had a spell of acting up at 12:30 this morning, pounding with his sneakers and hanging his clothes and blankets on the bars. Examination shows subject to be sitting quietly and fairly attentive, but answering questions hesitatingly and only after long pauses. He is disoriented for time and place; thinks he is in prison but does not know which one. He is not sure as to why he is there but thinks he might have been in some kind of trouble. He says that they claim he hit somebody. The stream of thought is very slow, interrupted, disconnected, and the subject is incapable of any sustained conversation. Memory is very poor for both recent and remote events. There is no disturbance in emotivity. I was unable to elicit the presence of any delusions or hallucinations. The neurological examination does not show any evidence of physical or neurological disease. The pupils are sluggish and the knee and ankle jerks are reduced. Joseph Williams is suffering from the dementing form of insanity. He should be transferred to a State Hospital for the Insane. The outlook for his recovery is very doubtful. Respectfully submitted, (signature illegible), Dr. E.M. Hammes and Dr. Joseph C. Michael."

J.J. Sullivan, Warden wrote the following letter to the State Board of Control on February 4, 1937: "Gentlemen: As authorized by the Board of Control, Joseph Williams was examined by a duly appointed sanity commission on February 3. He was adjudged insane, and has this day been committed to the Asylum for the Dangerously Insane at St. Peter. While we cannot rely on the information he gives, he claims to have a sister, Mrs. Ida Mulcahey at Pittsburgh, Kansas, and she has been notified of this change. Yours very truly, J.J. Sullivan, Warden."

On February 4, 1937, the warden wrote the following letter to Mrs. Ida Mulcahey: "Dear Madam: Because of the mental condition of your brother, Joseph Williams, it was deemed necessary to transfer him to the mental hospital at St. Peter, Minnesota. Inquiry as to his welfare should be sent to Dr. George H. Freeman, St. Peter, Minnesota. You will readily understand that this change has been made largely for the brother's benefit inasmuch as this institution is not properly equipped to handle mental cases. Yours very truly, J.J. Sullivan, Warden."

Joseph Williams spent twenty years, ten months, and two days in the state hospital. He suffered from pulmonary tuberculosis the last five years of his life and died on December 6, 1957. His body was taken to the University of Minnesota where it was cremated on December 9. There was no further information found regarding his family or his burial site.

The murdered victim remains unidentified to this day, but what still remains from this terrible tragedy is the brown leather wallet that the victim always kept with him. His identification, his photos, and his money are all long gone. This wallet was found along with Joseph Williams' court transcript file at the Minnesota History Center in St. Paul.

Joseph Williams, Stillwater Prison photo, inmate #13401
Photo from Minnesota Historical Society

CHARRED BODY FOUND

A TALL, SLENDER man, dressed in suit and tie and wearing a slouch hat, drove into the Omholt Phillips 66 Service Station in Sacred Heart about 6:45 on the evening of July 7, 1939 and asked for a quart of gasoline. Burnett Chelin, the seventeen-year-old attendant, was on duty while M.J. Omholt, proprietor, was home for supper. The stranger wanted the gas for a camp stove. He said he was camped in the tourist park, however, there is no tourist park in Sacred Heart.

"This gas is leaded and not suitable for a stove," Chelin said.

"I don't care," the stranger replied, "for I find leaded gas works better anyway."

Then Chelin drained three quarts into a two-gallon gas can before the stranger shouted, "Whoa, I only wanted a quart." Upon noticing the gas can, the stranger asked for an old bottle or oil can because he wouldn't be bringing the can back. Chelin found a five-quart oil can and the gas was emptied from the gas container into the oil can by the stranger. The stranger, who drove into the station from the west, drove away again headed west after paying Chelin 15 cents in correct change for the transaction.

Gordon Sheggeby, a farmer who lived near Sacred Heart, discovered a car in flames on the main gravel road between Sacred Heart and Echo. The car rested on the right-hand side of the road where it is customary to drive, and it was not on the shoulder. The scene was about a mile north of the Minnesota river on a winding road. Vision of the road ahead of the car was limited to a block and back of the car, less than three blocks—due to the curves. On the east side of the auto was a deeply wooded ravine. When Gordon arrived on the scene, he saw a head extending out over the cushion in the front seat. The passenger's side door of the 1939 Chevrolet coach was open. Flames and heat from the blazing car prevented Gordon from getting close to the auto and removing the body. He was attracted to the scene after members of the family heard a horn blowing steadily for fifteen minutes while they were eating supper, so he decided to investigate. A few minutes after Gordon arrived, his brother Owen came to the scene, enroute to Sacred Heart. Gordon remained at the scene while Owen drove to town to notify Officer Ole Dahl. Dahl telephoned Sheriff Henry Heaney immediately. Dr. D.R. Miller, county coroner of Bird Island, was contacted and arrived at the scene about 9 p.m.

While Gordon was watching the inferno, the body slumped off the seat and onto the running board, but the legs remained in the car. News of the burning car traveled fast throughout the rural community. Soon P.H. Paulson and Morrel Agre, who lived nearby, rushed to the scene with two large fire extinguishers, sprayed the liquid into the backseat of the vehicle, and were able to recover calling cards, contract papers, and other personal items.

The charred body was removed to the Nordstrom and Sagnes undertaking parlors and the completely demolished, heat-twisted car was towed into Kull's garage in Sacred Heart.

Rumors that the body was a woman's were squelched late that night when H.H. Lord, a Montevideo insurance man and longtime friend of the deceased, identified the body as that of Odin M. Norby. Lord was able to identify Norby by the small, odd-shaped filling in a front tooth.

Both legs and the left arm were burned off. A fracture was found on the left side of the head, but at the coroner's inquest, no decision was reached as to whether it came from a blow, a fall, or the intense heat.

John B. Burns, expert from the state bureau of criminal apprehension in Willmar, sifted the ashes in the car and besides a quarter coin, glass frames, car keys and personal keys, and a badly burned billfold, nothing of importance was found that might solve the case.

Although it was hinted that parts of the body, including a lung, would be sent to the University of Minnesota for further examination, the office of

Odin Norby, age 37
Photo from *Star Tribune*, July 9, 1939

J.M. Anderson, Chippewa county coroner, informed the newspaper that no part of the body was sent to the Twin Cities.

Norby was a collector for the Federal Discount Corporation with headquarters in Dubuque, Iowa, and worked out of Montevideo, which was an office of the Mankato branch. He had worked for the company for the past four years and was held in the highest regard by everyone. His employer, H.T. Aske, said Norby was an outstanding employee, his records were always in balance and correct in every detail. Norby had told his wife he was going to Morris on business that Friday morning. He was thirty-seven years old, survived by his wife Estelle and two daughters, aged eight and five. Funeral services were held on July 10 in Morris.

Few, if any, residents of Montevideo, who knew Norby believed it was suicide, nor did others who were acquainted with him. A motive for suicide had not been established and Norby was known for his congeniality, striking personality, and good character. With dozens of rumors floating around and numerous explanations being offered, the case remained clouded. Authorities withheld all findings on the case until they presented them to the jury.

Dr. M. Fawcett of Renville conducted an examination at the inquest on July 8 and explained that the fracture of the skull was a result of intense heat. There were numerous cracks around the hole in the skull, but none of them penetrated through the skull. The fracture was just above the ear and in the thinnest part of the skull. It measured three-fourths of an inch in diameter. Due to the severely burned condition of the body, it was impossible to examine the lungs to determine if life left the body before or during the burning. The stomach was too charred to permit further examination.

Dr. Dordal of Sacred Heart examined the remains and was of the same opinion as Dr. Fawcett, that the fracture resulted from intense heat. Dr. D.R. Miller, County Coroner of Bird Island, explained how heat could cause the fracture, inasmuch as it occurred in the thinnest part of the skull and was on the side subjected to the severest heat.

County Attorney Russell Frazee was in charge of the inquest. He was assisted by Coroner Dr. D.R. Miller of Bird Island and Attorney John C. Haave of Montevideo.

The coroner's jury trial was held on July 14. Due to the absence of a definite motive for suicide, interest in the case increased steadily the week preceding the trial, as many were of the opinion that Norby had been murdered. It was rumored that Norby's accounts were short, but authorities carefully guarded all the evidence until the trial opened. The village hall, scene of the sensational hearing, was filled to capacity. Thirteen witnesses testified in the trial which lasted two hours.

One of the witnesses, Lawrence Larson, employed as a grader operator on a road crew working northwest of Watson, stated he saw Norby at 11:30 a.m. on Friday, July 7. He stated he noticed the front fenders and bumpers damaged and the left running board and rear fender bashed in—the condition of Norby's car when found burning. Norby waved to Larson as he passed. The following day, Larson accompanied

Sheriff Heaney and Sheriff Peterson of Chippewa County to the area were Larson had worked that day. A short distance away, they found tire marks where a car had gone into the ditch, and about one-fourth of a mile further, they found tracks where a car had pulled out of the ditch and onto the road. These tracks were believed to be Norby's.

John Sagnes, a farmer living five miles southwest of Sacred Heart, testified that he, along with his daughter-in-law and granddaughters, went to the Minnesota River on a fishing trip that day. Enroute to the river, a car resembling Norby's followed them and then passed them. When the Sagnes family reached the river, the same car had crossed the bridge, turned around, and was parked facing north. Sagnes met the man (Norby) on the bridge and they carried on a conversation. Sagnes noticed Norby had a handful of stones and was tossing them into the river while inquiring as to the depth of the stream at that point. Other than this strange behavior, Norby appeared normal.

Burnett Chelin, the seventeen-year-old station attendant who sold a stranger 15 cents worth of gasoline, was another witness called to the stand. He identified three photos of Norby as being the party that bought the gasoline from him. The five-quart oil can that Norby took the gasoline in was found across the road in some weeds that same evening.

The most interesting and revealing testimony came from H.T. Aske, Norby's employer. He noted a discrepancy in Norby's accounts during the week preceding July 6, but after close investigation, found that the shortage dated back to December 8, 1938, when a $634 account of a motor company, which had been paid to Norby, did not clear through the Mankato branch. Checking further, Norby was found to be approximately $1100 short, (today valued at $20,223) whereupon Aske drove to Montevideo, Thursday, July 6 to discuss the situation with Norby. That evening, the two men spent several hours delving into the records and the following morning, Norby called Aske's hotel room, and informed him that he (Norby) was going to Morris that day to borrow sufficient money from his brothers-in-law (Watzke and Probst) to cover the shortage. Norby was forced to dip into the company's money, he told Aske, in order to "cover the expense of getting business." Aske said Norby's conduct during the discussion of the shortage was normal, except that Norby appeared more serious and quieter than usual. Aske was very surprised to hear the news at 3 a.m. Saturday that Norby's charred body was found in an automobile near Sacred Heart. Aske said no warrant for the arrest of Norby had been issued or even contemplated, and no threat against him had been made. Norby was bonded for $10,000.

After a short discussion of the case by Coroner Miller, the jury, made up of J.H. Paulson, A.N. Stenborg, O.C. Sparstad, M.J. Omholt, A.G. Siewert and G.P. Mangerud, retired for five minutes and then brought in a verdict of death by suicide.

Considerable interest was aroused before and after the trial when a representative of a large insurance company displayed photos of a similar case which took place in McIntosh, South Dakota in 1938. Like the Norby case, a Ford V-8 coupe was completely destroyed by fire and its owner, C.E. Richards, was burned to death in the car. Richards was murdered and the payroll he carried was stolen. The insurance man was here to seek a possible connection between the Norby and South Dakota tragedies, but the relationship was dismissed when the coroner's jury rendered a verdict of suicide. The following letter from Richard's widow appeared in the *Sacred Heart News* dated July 20, 1939. The local newspaper story attracted the attention of Mrs. C.E. Richards of Muscatine, Iowa, and Ole Dahl, local police officer, received the following letter from there:

1614 Mulberry Ave.
Muscatine, Iowa
July 10, 1939
Chief of Police,

Dear Sir:
In the Chicago Herald Examiner of Sunday, July 9 was an item about the finding of the burned body of O.M. Norby of Montevideo, Minn., saying he was found with a fractured skull in

his burning automobile.

On Nov. 2, 1938, my husband, E.E. Richards of McIntosh, South Dakota, met his death in what seems an identical manner. He was found the next morning badly burned in his burned car and had a fractured skull. He was a contractor and builder and was supervising a government project of six homes in Standing Rock Indian Reservation. He was carrying the payroll, but the payment to his men was made by check and the briefcase containing them was found some 250 feet from the burned car.

To date, no trace of the murderer has been found so when I read the statement of this similar death, I thought the same person might be at work again. I have written our sheriff of Corson county and our county attorney, asking them to communicate with you hoping reciprocal information might prove helpful to both cases. It seems to me some ring might be working out of Minneapolis or St. Paul.

I am enclosing a self-addressed envelope with the request that you send me any information that can be given out, for you can understand, I'm sure, how anxious I am that anyone you apprehend be questioned in our case too, if there is any possible excuse for so doing.

Yours Truly, (Mrs. C.E.) Frances Richards

It was estimated that thousands of people viewed the fire-gutted auto stored at Kull's garage in Sacred Heart. People swarmed into the building during the first few days, but even two weeks later, there were still a few from surrounding towns that came to see the wreck.

Sacred Heart received an enormous amount of publicity throughout the United States as a result of the Norby case. The Minneapolis office of the Associated Press (AP), which serves newspapers across the country, picked up the story and relayed it by telegraph to thousands of papers as a piece of "hot" news. The AP kept the long-distance wires burning between Minneapolis and Sheriff Heaney, Coroner Miller,

Charred remains of Norby's 1939 Chevrolet Coach
Photo from *Sacred Heart News*, July 13, 1939

Harry Sagnes (the undertaker) in an effort to keep up on the story. AP also sent a picture of Norby's car to Chicago and New York, and it was run in dozens of the metropolitan newspapers in connection with the story. This case had all the earmarks of a BIG story.

It appeared that this was not the end of the Norby case. Relatives and close friends were dissatisfied with the coroner's jury verdict of suicide on July 14. No postmortem was performed on July 8, the day following the tragedy, but Coroner Dr. D.R. Miller told the newspaper that the entire interior of Norby's mouth—tongue, gums, roof and cheeks—were burned severely. Norby's family felt an autopsy should have been performed, since there could have been a possibility of foul play. W.W. Watzke and H.C. Probst, brothers-in-law of Norby, who resided in Morris, contacted Dr. J.S. MaCartney, professor of pathology and anatomy at the University of Minnesota, to perform a postmortem examination on the remains. Dr. MaCartney was a well-known expert called by insurance companies for investigations into suspicious deaths. On July 18, Norby's body was disinterred at Morris, and Dr. MaCartney, assisted by Montevideo physicians, performed the autopsy. The bronchial tubes, one lung, and the heart were among the organs removed and taken to the university for analysis. After a close examination, the body was again buried. MaCartney's report would go to the state bureau of criminal apprehension, and the bureau, together with Frazee, would decide whether the new evidence warranted the reopening of the case.

Both Frazee and Miller remained firm in their belief that Norby took his own life, judging from all of the evidence presented at the trial, but were willing to listen to any new testimony that might be obtained. Not a single word nor hint was given by any of the witnesses at the trial that Norby might have been the victim of foul play or murder.

Excerpts from MaCartney's report were as follows: "It is my opinion from the findings in the body that Mr. Norby was dead before he was burned. This opinion is based on the fact that there was no carbon in the trachea or bronchi and no evidence of carbon monoxide poisoning as indicated by the color of the tissues which had not been destroyed by fire. Just how the injury to the head was sustained, I am not in a position to say, but I believe that it was the immediate cause of death."

Norby's skull revealed two fractures in the back of the head in addition to one just above the ear on the left side, but these were attributed to heat. A blood clot at the base of Norby's brain, containing two and one-half ounces of blood, came from a blow, according to Dr. MaCartney, while other physicians, in comparing the condition with others in medical history, say the clot need not necessarily come from a blow.

Fresh evidence had been supplied by Norby's friends and relatives since the exhumation, but no new clues had been found that might indicate Norby met with foul play. Other than the $1100 shortage in Norby's accounts, no motive for suicide had been found.

By August 1939, evidence pointing more and more conclusively to suicide in the Norby case was being uncovered by local and state authorities, who were still working daily on the mystery. An auditor for the Federal Discount Corporation of Dubuque, Iowa was requested to do an intensive survey of all Norby's accounts and found additional shortages that amounted to $5,486.30 (today valued at $100,858), nearly five times the original amount of $1,100.

And there was the refutation, in part, of Dr. MaCartney's report on his finding in the case. Many points brought out in Dr. MaCartney's lengthy report were not satisfactorily detailed and explained according to County Attorney Frazee and Burns, and a conference was scheduled to get a better understanding of the postmortem.

A blood clot containing two and one-half ounces of blood was found at the base of Norby's brain, the report stated, and could result only from a blow on the head, but at the conference, the pathologist said he found, upon checking similar cases in medical history, that it was common to find blood clots caused from hemorrhages, in bodies that had been burned to death.

Two holes were found in the back of the head, which at first indicated foul play, but Dr. MaCartney stated they were caused from burning, as there was "no injury to the brain. They could not have been fractures, he added, because no lines or cracks could be found radiating from the holes."

Asked why he stated in his report his belief that "Norby was dead before he burned," Dr. MaCartney said the information furnished him on the case by the relatives, plus the circumstances, and plus the condition of the respiratory organs led him to that opinion.

However, the physician remained firm in that part of his report that read "…there was no carbon in the trachea or bronchi and no evidence of carbon monoxide poisoning as indicated by the color of the tissues which had not been destroyed by fire." This statement meant little, in the opinion of local authorities, because there is no way of knowing whether a person burning to death has to inhale the hot fumes and flames for one second, one minute, five minutes, or whether the explosion occurring when gasoline is ignited renders the body immediately lifeless or not.

"Judging from the circumstances I had, together with the findings," Dr. MaCartney said that "it was a reasonable assumption that Norby was dead before burning, but now after hearing the full details of the case, it is only reasonable to assume that it was a suicide case."

Although the case was not closed, it appeared doubtful that a new hearing would be held. No new clues had been found that indicated Norby had been murdered on the evening of July 7.

On August 3, 1939, County Attorney Russell Frazee and John Burns discovered the spot on a road near Morris where Norby drove into the ditch, damaging his car. It was brought out at the coroner's jury hearing that Norby was believed to have bashed the front end and side of his car in a ditch near Watson. But Norby drove off a 12-foot embankment near Morris, according to Frazee, and plowed through a five-wire fence into a flax field. His car suddenly changed its course in the field, as if the wheels had "jack-knifed," and rammed through another five-wire fence. He then drove about 300 feet through a pasture and dropped down a six-foot grade to get back on the highway. Four guard posts supporting a guide wire were snapped off by Norby when he left the highway. His speed must have been 70 or 80 miles an hour when he plowed off the 12-foot embankment, or his car would have rolled over several times.   Although no one saw the car leave the road, authorities were positive it was Norby's auto because upon digging around in the flax field, they found a small part of a car that they found missing on Norby's automobile. Another piece of evidence found was a piece of wood tightly wedged in the front spring of Norby's car that matched the wood in one of the guard posts which was snapped off. County Attorney Frazee completed his investigation in September, and without any new evidence discovered to indicate foul play, Norby's death was declared a suicide.

Estelle Norby, along with her two daughters, Joann and Louise, moved to Morris, Minnesota shortly after her husband's death. She was employed in the office of a lumberyard, a position she held before her marriage.

Action was started for Mrs. Norby by a group of her husband's friends, and the case was heard before a referee in Morris in late November 1939. The trial was continued until January 10, 1940, but the preceding day the insurance company offered to settle the case for $3,250. The offer was accepted, although the state set the value of a life at $7,500, if payments were extended over a period of months, or a lump settlement of $5,250. In February 1940, Estelle Norby was awarded $3,250 in settlement of the employer's compensation insurance policy which covered her husband. The suicide verdict was somewhat discredited by the State of Minnesota Industrial Commission. Compensation insurance is required of every employer in Minnesota and covers employees who are injured or killed while performing their duties. Norby's status was that of an employee of the Federal Discount Insurance Corporation. Compensation insurance is voided in the event of suicide; hence the suicide verdict did not hold with the Industrial Commission, nor the insurance company.

After this settlement, O.K. Alger, Morris attorney, hired by Mrs. Norby, started investigating a $5,000 Prudential Life Insurance Company policy of Norby's which, in the event of accidental death, would pay double indemnity--$10,000. An unusual clause in the policy delayed payment of the insurance for one year, and would not be due until July 7, 1940, exactly twelve months after Norby's death. If the Prudential company refused to accept the cause of Norby's death as accidental, it was hinted that action would be started. It was quite possible that the case would be reopened later in district court in Olivia, at which time the local coroner's jury would be recalled to hear new evidence and reconsider the case.

(Special Note: In checking with the Renville County Court administrator's office in May 2019, it appeared no civil cases were ever reopened relating to this matter for the years 1939 through 1942. It could not be determined if Mrs. Norby received $10,000, double indemnity from the Prudential Life Insurance Company for her husband's death. On the Find a Grave website for Odin Norby, it stated that a prime suspect in this case had a heart attack and died before he could be prosecuted, but no further information could be located to confirm this.)

It appeared Norby had been embezzling money from his employer, and when it was discovered, Norby couldn't find a way out of his predicament. He had tarnished his good reputation and brought shame and embarrassment to his family. He came up with a plan to commit suicide but attempted to make it look like an accident so his wife could collect the $10,000 double-indemnity policy from the Prudential Insurance Company. I guess we will never know all the particulars of what really happened on July 7, 1939, and Norby's death will forever remain a mystery.

Odin Norby Marker from Find a Grave
Summit Cemetery, Morris, Minnesota

HACKED IN BED

OTTILIE WENDTLAND WAS born on August 29, 1888 to parents, Wilhelm and Bertha. There were seven children in the family with Ottilie (aka Tillie) being the fourth in line. She was nineteen years old when she married Carl Lindeman in 1908. Carl was born on November 7, 1880 to parents Carl and Emelia. He had five siblings and was the fourth one born. Carl and Tillie had one daughter, Gladys, born in 1912. They lived on a farm in Renville County for over twenty years. In 1938, Mr. Lindeman sold his 120-acre farm seven miles north of Hector and moved into the old "Cook" house just beyond the Hector city limits on the west side of town. He was known as a moderately well-to-do man and was careful with his money.

Carl Lindeman was considered an industrious and peaceful old man. He never seemed to have trouble with anyone. He had improved the appearance of his property, by painting the house, cutting down trees and landscaping the yard. He had planned to dig a basement for the house and make it appear more modern. He drove a Model T Ford, of a year about 1924, which was kept spic-and-span.

A murder was discovered on Tuesday, April 2, 1940 about 8 a.m. when Mrs. Lindeman appeared at the home of Rev. C.M. Anderson, a neighbor, saying her husband was dead and asking the family to call the police. Upon investigation, Carl Lindeman was found fully clothed, lying on the bed in the second-floor bedroom, which faced east. He had been struck about the head three times with an ax.

Rev. Anderson called Ed Butler, the village policeman and deputy sheriff, who then notified Sheriff Heaney and County Attorney Russell Frazee. They arrived on the scene in a few minutes, shortly before 9 a.m. Dr. D.R. Miller, county coroner, was also notified. Dr. Miller estimated the slaying occurred between six or seven in the morning. Mrs. Lindeman had mopped blood from the floor in the bedroom before going to the neighbor's house. "I found him dead in bed; that's all I know about it." said Mrs. Lindeman.

Officials found that the body was still warm, and fully clothed, which led them to believe that Lindeman had arisen, had breakfast and had laid down again and was then attacked. The floor of the bedroom was found scrubbed clean and the ax, discovered later behind a door in the chicken coop, was also cleaned, save for the butt of the handle where some blood, flesh, and hair were found. The pail, presumably used for cleaning, was found in the kitchen. Fresh footprints were found leading to the ax. County Attorney Frazee said that water had been used to wash the blood from the ax and that the water had been thrown on the grass and snow. A pair of blood-stained ladies' overshoes were also found by the authorities. Officers said Mrs. Lindeman would not explain her delay in notifying someone of the death. "I don't know," was her reply to almost every question.

Sherman D. Taylor, a son-in-law of the Lindemans, told authorities of family troubles and that Ottilie had threatened to kill herself and her husband on several occasions. Rumor had it that she had made threats in the past that she intended on killing her husband, and that

Lindeman house, chicken coop in left background
Photo courtesy Renville County Historical Society

Chicken Coop where ax was found behind a door
Photo courtesy Renville County Historical Society

(Special Note: the two photos above are from the collection of actual crime scene photos taken by investigators at the scene on April 2, 1940. These were found in a file at the Renville County Museum, along with the ax used in the murder. The evidence photos were going to be destroyed, but Donald Walser took possession of them and donated the photos to the Renville County Historical Society on November 8, 1983.)

she was considered somewhat demented.

The body was taken to Hutchinson where an autopsy was performed. The victim's vital organs were taken by Mr. Heaney and Mr. Frazee to the University for examination by scientists, making an effort to determine whether some poisons had been used.

Mr. Lindeman's body was taken charge of by his only daughter, Gladys, and son-in-law, Sherman Taylor, who lived in Boon Lake Township about 13 miles northeast of Hector. The funeral was held on Saturday, April 6 at 2 p.m. at St. Paul's Lutheran Church in Hector. He was buried in the Hector City Cemetery. He was sixty years old at the time of death.

The sole suspect, Ottilie Lindeman, was held at the county jail in Olivia, but although questioned repeatedly by County Attorney Frazee and Sheriff Heaney, she refused to admit any knowledge of the crime. During brief questioning, Frazee said Mrs. Lindeman repeatedly screamed, "I didn't do it," before she nearly collapsed and a physician was summoned to quiet her.

Mrs. Lindeman was under continued surveillance of a matron guard. During further questioning the following week, she admitted remembering the washing of the ax and hiding it in the chicken coop and throwing the water on the ground, north of the house, but she still denied any knowledge of the gruesome deed, and stated, "If I killed him, I don't remember doing it."

A special grand jury was in session in the courthouse at Olivia on April 17. County Attorney Frazee presented evidence in the case of Ottilie Lindeman charged with the murder of her husband. Mr. Frazee stated that if an indictment was returned, he would file it with the court subject to an insanity hearing, which would then be called. Mrs. Lindeman had been in a hysterical condition ever since she was committed to the county jail. Later that day, the grand jury indicted Mrs. Lindeman for first-degree murder.

Following the grand jury's action, the woman's attorney, D.S. Lane of Olivia, moved for a sanity hearing under a section of the law which provides that the district court may order the defendant committed to an insane asylum where it is found that the defendant is insane at the time of the hearing, without considering the mental status of the defendant at the time of the commission of the crime. If later released from the St. Peter institution, Mrs. Lindeman would be tried on a charge of murder.

A sanity hearing was held on April 19 for Mrs. Lindeman. Present at the hearing were Dr. G.H. Mesker of Olivia, Dr. F.W. Penhall of Morton and Dr. W.H. Hengstler of St. Paul for the defendant; and for the state, Dr. J.A. Cosgriff of Olivia and Dr. Magnus C. Peterson of the Willmar State Hospital. The order of the court stated she would be kept in the institution "for safekeeping and treatment and that said defendant shall there remain and be cared for until she shall recover and be restored to her right mind, when she shall be returned to this court to be dealt with according to law and to answer the charge of murder in the first degree now pending in this court against her."

At the conclusion of the sanity hearing, it was determined that Mrs. Lindeman was declared insane. Judge Quale signed the commitment papers, and she was committed to the asylum for the insane at St. Peter on April 22, 1940. Many years later, Ottilie was transferred to Ah Gwah Ching nursing home from the asylum. She passed away there on August 20, 1968 and was buried next to Carl in the Hector City Cemetery. She was seventy-nine years old at time of death.

(Special Note: We searched for Ottilie's St. Peter asylum records at the Minnesota History Center, but since Ottilie was deceased, the index card was marked "Death Case Destroyed," so we were unable to find out what kind of a life she lived in the insane asylum. She never recovered from her mental illness and therefore, was never prosecuted for the murder of her husband.)

One can only imagine what caused Ottilie to viciously attack her husband with an ax while he slept. Was she a victim of domestic violence, was she severely depressed, or was she suffering from some other mental aberration? We will never know for sure what happened in the early morning hours of April 2, 1940 in the Lindeman household so many years ago.

Carl & Ottilie Lindeman markers
Hector City Cemetery, Hector, Minnesota
Photos by author

REFERENCES

RENVILLE COUNTY HISTORY

History of Renville County, MN by Franklin Curtiss-Wedge, Vol. II, pub. 1916 pgs. 275-276 and Wikipedia

JOSEPH RENVILLE

History of Renville County, MN by Franklin Curtiss-Wedge, Vol. II, pub. 1916 pgs. 82-87 and Wikipedia

FIRST LAWSUIT IN RENVILLE COUNTY

History of Renville County, MN by Franklin Curtiss-Wedge, Vol. II, pub. 1916 pgs. 1353-1354

INCESTUOUS RAPE

District Court records—9th Judicial District, filed December 9, 1878, State of Minnesota vs. Henry Knauf

"St. Peter Letter," The Saint Paul Globe, December 25, 1878, pg. 2

"Cox's Court," The Saint Paul Globe, January 18, 1879, pg. 1

MICHAEL J. DOWLING

Progressive Men of Minnesota, pg. 163

The Things We Know Best by Joe Paddock, pub. 1976 "Dowling Just Wouldn't Give Up," pgs. 234-241

Michael J. Dowling School website and Wikipedia

WIFE SLAYER

Probate Court records, General Term, October 3, 1881, Insanity Hearing

"Broke Jail," Renville Times, March 9, 1882, pg. 3

Arrest Warrant, March 15, 1882

New Ulm Review, March 22, 1882, pg. 3

The Saint Paul Globe, July 27, 1882, pg. 3

The Saint Paul Globe, December 16, 1882, pg. 15

State of Minnesota Executive Department, Commute Sentence, July 8, 1891

SHOT IN THE HEAD

District Court records—9th Judicial District, filed November 29, 1882, State of Minnesota vs. William Eagan

"Eagan's Confession," Star Tribune, November 23, 1882, pg. 1

"Murder in Renville County," New Ulm Review, November 29, 1882, pg. 3

State of Minnesota Executive Department, Pardon, December 29, 1892

FELL IN A WELL

District Court records—State of Minnesota vs. Ole Rogn, May14, 1884

New Ulm Review, February 27, 1884

"A Renville County Murderer Arrested," Little Falls Transcript, February 29, 1884

New Ulm Review, March 5, 1884

A FAMILY FEUD

District Court records—State of Minnesota vs. Lincoln H. Parker, October 12, 1888

"Lawyer W.C. White," Star Tribune, August 2, 1888, pg. 8

New Ulm Review, August 8, 1888, pg. 2

"Parker Goes Scot-Free," The Saint Paul Globe, October 18, 1888, pg. 1

BULLETS AND POISON

"Cowardly Murder," The Morton Enterprise, November 16, 1894, pg. 1

"The Otto Murder," The Morton Enterprise, November 23, 1894, pg. 4

"Poisoned and Shot," The Morton Enterprise, November 30, 1894, pg. 4

"A Scandalous Article," The Morton Enterprise, December 7, 1894, pg. 4

"Emanuel Otto Shot by an Unknown Hand," The Morton Enterprise, January 18, 1895, pg. 4

"Emanuel Otto Murdered," Redwood Reveille, November 17, 1894, pg. 5

"The Otto Murder," Redwood Reveille, November 24, 1894, pg. 1

"Poison," Redwood Reveille, December 1, 1894, pg. 1

"A Renville County Crime," Redwood Gazette, November 15, 1894, pg. 1

"The Deed of a Dastard!" Redwood Gazette, November 22, 1894, pg. 1

"With Poison and Bullets," Redwood Gazette, November 29, 1894, pg. 1

"Mystery Still," Redwood Gazette, December 6, 1894, pg. 1

"Give it Up," Redwood Gazette, December 13, 1894, pg. 1

"Otto was Poisoned," Minneapolis Journal, November 27, 1894, pg. 1

"Who Murdered Otto," Minneapolis Journal, December 3, 1894, pg. 1

BURNED ALIVE

"Burned in His Cell," Redwood Gazette, November 9, 1897, pg. 3

VIOLENTLY INSANE

"Violently Insane," Olivia Times, January 29, 1903, pg. 1

GONE INSANE

"Goes Insane," Olivia Times, April 23, 1903, pg. 4

ROBBERY AT DANUBE

"Bold Robbery at Danube," Olivia Times, October 8, 1908, pg. 1

"Bank Robbers Visit Danube," Renville Star Farmer, October 9, 1908, pg. 1

"Bank Broken Into," Franklin Tribune, October 9, 1908, pg. 1

"Danube Bank Robbed," Bird Island Union, October 9, 1908, pg. 1

DOUBLE MURDER AND SUICIDE

"Murder and Suicide in Triple Tragedy," Olivia Times, August 10, 1911, pg. 1

"Olivia Scene of Horrible Double Murder and Suicide," Bird Island Union, August 10, 1911, pg. 1

"A Tragedy at Olivia," Franklin Tribune, August 11, 1911, pg. 1

"A Double Murder at Olivia Horrified the Community," Willmar Tribune, August 16, 1911, pg. 5

CRAZY MAN

"Terrible Acts of Insane Man," Olivia Times, December 28, 1911, pg. 1

"Fred Zaske Burns Barn," Bird Island Union, December 28, 1911, pg. 1

"Demented Man Commits Suicide," Olivia Times, November 21, 1918, pg. 1

"Fred Zaske Attempts to Kill His Wife," Bird Island Union, November 28, 1918, pg. 1

"Fred Zaske Hangs Himself After Terrible Act," Redwood Gazette, November 27, 1918, pg. 2

"Olivia Man Attempts Murder," Willmar Tribune, November 27, 1918, pg. 7

BOXCAR MURDER

"Bird Island Murder Case," Olivia Times, September 11, 1913, pg. 1

"Brookfield Farmer Killed in Boxcar," Bird Island Union, September 11, 1913, pg. 1

"Brookfield Man Shot," The Morton Enterprise, September 12, 1913, pg. 1

"Minnesota Farmer Killed in Boxcar," Renville Star Farmer, September 12, 1913, pg. 2

"Obituary—Willie O. Olson," The Hector Mirror, September 12, 1913, pg. 1

TUBERCULOSIS SANATORIUM

Riverside Sanatorium at Granite Falls, Minnesota, website

MURDER AND SUICIDE

"Unbalanced Mind Cause of Murder and Suicide," The Morton Enterprise, January 12, 1917, pg. 1

"Shoots Daughter Then Kills Self," Renville Star Farmer, January 17, 1917, pg. 1

"A Terrible Tragedy Enacted at Morton," The Lamberton Star, January 19, 1917, pg. 1

"Awful Tragedy Near Morton," Willmar Tribune, January 24, 1917, pg. 1

DEADLY SHOOTING

"Schoepke Case Will go to Jurymen Today," Granite Falls Tribune, May 18, 1932, pg. 1

"Brothers Engage in Brawl," Sacred Heart News, Feb. 18, 1932

"Argument Over Rifle," Renville newspaper, Feb. 25, 1932

"Court Convened for Duty Monday," Sacred Heart News, May 12, 1932

"Hawk Creek Farmer Killed by Gun Shots Inflicted by Brother," Sacred Heart News, February 25, 1932, pg. 1

"Schoepke Rites Held Thursday," Sacred Heart News, March 3, 1932, pg. 1

"Slayer Tries to Escape from County Jail," Sacred Heart News, April 14, 1932, pg. 6

"Murder Trial on in Court," Sacred Heart News, May 19, 1932, pg. 1

"Schoepke Sentenced to Prison for Life," Sacred Heart News, May 26, 1932 pg. 1

The Post-Crescent, November 22, 1911, pg. 6

Wausau Daily Herald, January 15, 1912, pg. 3

Wausau Daily Herald, May 17, 1913, pg. 2

Wausau Daily Herald, July 28, 1922, pg. 2

District Court records—12th Judicial District, State of Minnesota vs. Paul Schoepke, May 9, 1932

Stillwater State Prison Records and death certificate, register No. 11212

MURDER ON THE RAILROAD TRACKS

"Man is Killed by Train," Sacred Heart News, September 17, 1936, pg. 1

"Man in Custody at Huron, Has Money of Local Suicide," Sacred Heart News, September 24, 1936, pg. 1

"Joe Williams Held at the County Jail," Sacred Heart News, October 1, 1936, pg. 1

"Admits Murder of Man Found Dead on Track," Sacred Heart News, October 8, 1936, pg. 1

"Transient Gets Life Sentence to Stillwater," Sacred Heart News, December 31, 1936, pg. 1

District Court records—12th Judicial District, State of Minnesota vs. Joseph Williams, October 7, 1936

Stillwater State Prison Records and death certificate, register No. 13401

CHARRED BODY FOUND

"Mystery Shrouds Montevideo Man's Death in Flaming Auto," Sacred Heart News, July 13, 1939, pg. 1

"O.M. Norby's Body Exhumed at Morris," Sacred Heart News, July 20, 1939, pg. 1

"Few Developments in Norby Case," Sacred Heart News, July 27, 1939, pg. 1

"U Pathologist's Report on Norby Case Shaken," Sacred Heart News, August 3, 1939, pg. 1

"Developments Few in Norby Matter," Sacred Heart News, August 10, 1939, pg. 1

"Norby Shortage Mounting as Probe Continues," Sacred Heart News, August 24, 1939, pg. 1

"Norby Shortage Has Increased," Granite Falls Tribune, August 17, 1939, pg. 1

"Sheriff Probes Mystery Death of O.M. Norby," Mankato Free Press, July 8, 1939, pg. 1

"Coroner Jury Visits Torch Death Scene," Star Tribune, July 9, 1939, pg. 1

"Auto Death is Named Suicide," St. Cloud Times, July 15, 1939, pg. 1

"Insurance Payment Shakes Verdict of Suicide in O.M. Norby Death," Sacred Heart News, February 8, 1940, pg. 1

HACKED IN BED

"Hector Man is Killed with Ax," Renville County Journal, April 4, 1940, pg. 1

"I Don't Remember Killing Him," Renville County Journal, April 11, 1940, pg. 1

"Grand Jury is Now in Session on Murder Case," Renville County Journal, April 18, 1940, pg. 1

"Mrs. Lindeman is Declared Insane," Renville County Journal, April 25, 1940, pg. 1

"Hector Man Believed Murdered," Bird Island Union, April 4, 1940, pg. 1

MURDER and MADNESS

"Hector Woman Committed to St. Peter Hospital," Bird Island Union, April 25, 1940, pg. 1

"Carl W. Lindeman Killed with Ax," Hector Mirror, April 9, 1940, pg. 1

"Grand Jury Indicts Mrs. Lindeman for Murder," Hector Mirror, April 18, 1940, pg. 1

"Hector Man Slain by Ax," Olivia Times, April 4, 1940, pg. 1

"Special Jury to be Called," Olivia Times, April 11, 1940, pg. 1

"Mrs. C. Lindeman Committed to Asylum," Olivia Times, April 25, 1940, pg. 1

"Hector Woman Faces First Degree Murder Charges," Sacred Heart News, April 11, 1940, pg. 1

"Murder Suspect is Placed in Asylum," St. Cloud Times, April 22, 1940, pg. 1

"Hector Man Slain by Ax Tuesday Morning," Olivia Times, April 4, 1940, pg. 1

ACKNOWLEDGEMENTS

MANY PEOPLE MUST be thanked in helping me compile the stories in this book. I am particularly indebted to my research specialist, Debra Gangelhoff, who spent numerous hours at the Minnesota History Center gathering information and discovering actual items used as evidence at the trials. I couldn't have completed this task without her help. A special thank you is extended to her in helping me develop the stories. She is a source of inspiration and encouragement during the project. Debra is an amazing person, and I can't thank her enough for all that she does for me.

Much gratitude is extended to the librarians at the Redwood and Renville Libraries where I'm allowed to spend numerous hours going through reels of microfilm looking for stories that may prove interesting. It all starts with finding intriguing stories in the old newspapers and then the real research begins.

I'm indebted to the historical societies who dedicate their time and talent in locating information and photos that add so much to the story. They are a great resource and a big thank you is extended to the staff at the following locations: Minnesota History Center,

Renville County Historical Society, and Sacred Heart Area Historical Society.

I also spend time in the archival rooms of newspaper offices, perusing the old newspapers. Thank you to the staff at the Redwood Gazette and Advocate Tribune newspaper offices for allowing me to spend time going through the old newspapers. It is always more enjoyable to read the newspaper than to try and find the story on a roll of microfilm.

A special thank you to the Renville County Court Administrator's office who helped me locate court case file numbers and probate records. A big thank you to Lara Szypszak, Reference Librarian at the Library of Congress who searched for information in the Pinkerton's National Detective Agency Records.

Joan Rogers, my copy editor, thank you so much for making sure the manuscript is at it's best, free from grammatical errors. You do such an amazing job and it's a pleasure to work with you. And to my publisher, Outskirts Press, a big thank you to all the staff involved in the publishing process. Thank you so much for your continued support.

Another important part of the story is locating the gravesites. I like to visit the final resting place of the victims, pay my respects, and put closure to their stories. I must thank the following people for helping me locate some of these gravesites: Derik at Dirks-Blem Funeral Home in Olivia, Jen Beckler, Deputy Clerk, City of Hector, and Jody Scholla and Becca Blumhoefer; two women who just happened to be driving around in the Hector City Cemetery the day I was there, and were kind enough to help me locate a couple of gravesites.

A special thank you to friends and acquaintances that give tidbits of information or take the time to show me the location where the crime took place. It makes the story real for me, when I can stand at the site of the crime and imagine what took place there so many years ago. I want to thank all my readers who have a passion for history and enjoy reading my books. I hope you like the book.

I look for all the missing pieces of the story and I write about what I find. Sometimes there's lots of information uncovered, but other times, not much can be found. It's an amazing adventure and every story is different. What was once lost but now is found, always remains a real treasure.

ABOUT THE AUTHOR

PATRICIA LUBECK WAS born in the small town of Echo, Yellow Medicine County, in southwestern Minnesota. She graduated from Echo High School and moved to Minneapolis, Minnesota in 1969. She attended the University of Minnesota for about a year, and then moved to California a few years later. She completed her associate degree at Ventura College, Ventura, California, and transferred to the University of California, Santa Barbara where she received her bachelor of arts degree with a major in interdisciplinary studies. Patricia returned to Minnesota in 2005 to take care of her elderly parents. She was hired as director of the Yellow Medicine County Museum in 2006 and later became the director of the Redwood County Museum in 2009. She retired from the position in 2018. Now she spends time traveling all over the country. She enjoys writing true crime stories that occurred in Minnesota in the nineteenth and twentieth centuries. Read her other books: Murder in Gales, A Rose Hanged Twice; Murder, Mystery and Mayhem in Minnesota; Crime and Calamity in Yellow Medicine County, Minnesota.

Check out her website at:
www.outskirtspress.com/MurderandMadness.

Patricia Lubeck

CPSIA information can be obtained
at www.ICGtesting.com
Printed in the USA
FFHW010901051119
55934235-61792FF